What's in Math Practice at Home?

The idea behind *Math Practice at Home* is simple and straightforward—frequent, focused practice leads to mastery and retention of the skills practiced.

The math practice is based on current standards and is designed to help your child understand math. The work should be done over several months. While the book includes a comprehensive set of second-grade skills, your child may be introduced to additional concepts in the classroom.

- Ten units
  Each unit includes 12 colorful pages of math practice.
  Units get progressively harder. Unit 10 is a review.

- Assessment pages
  After every two units, an assessment page tests your child's understanding of the topics covered in the units. The final assessment is two pages.

- Practice cards
  Card stock flash cards provide practice in basic math facts. After you have completed this book, use the flash cards to maintain the skills developed.

What Skills Are Included?

- Read, write, and compare numbers to 1,000
- Addition & subtraction facts to 18
- Two-digit addition with & without regrouping
- Two-digit subtraction with & without regrouping
- Three-digit addition & subtraction without regrouping
- Multiplication facts to 25
- Identify and continue patterns
- Value of pennies, nickels, dimes, quarters, dollar bills
- Solve word problems
- Geometry—basic shapes, symmetry, perimeter
- Tell time to the hour and half hour
- Identify fractions—$\frac{1}{2}$, $\frac{1}{3}$, $\frac{1}{4}$, $\frac{3}{4}$, $\frac{2}{3}$, $\frac{1}{6}$, $\frac{1}{8}$
- Read and create graphs and diagrams
- Measure to the nearest half inch

How to Use Math Practice at Home

Provide Time

Make sure that your child has a quiet time for practice. The practice session should be short and successful. Consider your child's personality and other activities as you decide how to schedule daily practice periods.

Provide Materials

Your child will need a quiet place to work. Put extra paper, scissors, crayons, pencils, and a glue stick in a tub or a box. To aid your child with computation, you may want to provide counters and a ruler to use as a number line. Store the supplies and *Math Practice at Home* in the work area you and your child choose.

Provide Encouragement and Support

Read instructions as needed. If your child needs help, talk about ways that a problem might be solved. Your response is important to your child's feelings of success. Keep your remarks positive. Recognize the effort your child has made. Correct mistakes together. Work toward independence, guiding practice when necessary.

Track Progress

After every two units, there is an assessment page entitled "I Can Do It!" (The final assessment in the book is two pages.) Your child should be able to successfully complete these assessments. If one skill seems to be a problem, review it before moving forward.

Pull-out Flash Cards

Pages 145–160 contain 96 addition and subtraction facts flash cards. The goal of flash card practice is for your child to commit the number facts to memory. Children vary dramatically in the ease and speed with which this goal is accomplished.

The 96 flash cards contain most of the addition and subtraction facts presented in the book. See page 144 for instructions on using the cards.

Ready, Set, Relay!

Follow the arrows to race through the problems.
Go this way.

$$\begin{array}{r} 2 \\ + 3 \\ \hline \end{array}$$
$$\begin{array}{r} 4 \\ + 1 \\ \hline \end{array}$$
$$\begin{array}{r} 1 \\ + 5 \\ \hline \end{array}$$
$$\begin{array}{r} 5 \\ + 4 \\ \hline \end{array}$$

$$\begin{array}{r} 1 \\ + 4 \\ \hline \end{array}$$
$$\begin{array}{r} 2 \\ + 4 \\ \hline \end{array}$$
$$\begin{array}{r} 5 \\ + 0 \\ \hline \end{array}$$
$$\begin{array}{r} 2 \\ + 2 \\ \hline \end{array}$$

$$\begin{array}{r} 4 \\ + 2 \\ \hline \end{array}$$
$$\begin{array}{r} 4 \\ + 6 \\ \hline \end{array}$$
$$\begin{array}{r} 5 \\ + 2 \\ \hline \end{array}$$
$$\begin{array}{r} 7 \\ + 2 \\ \hline \end{array}$$

$$\begin{array}{r} 5 \\ + 5 \\ \hline \end{array}$$
$$\begin{array}{r} 4 \\ + 3 \\ \hline \end{array}$$
$$\begin{array}{r} 4 \\ + 4 \\ \hline \end{array}$$
$$\begin{array}{r} 3 \\ + 7 \\ \hline \end{array}$$

$$\begin{array}{r} 3 \\ + 2 \\ \hline \end{array}$$
$$\begin{array}{r} 0 \\ + 3 \\ \hline \end{array}$$
$$\begin{array}{r} 3 \\ + 5 \\ \hline \end{array}$$
$$\begin{array}{r} 4 \\ + 5 \\ \hline \end{array}$$

Field Day Fun

Shot Put

Six contestants took part in a shot put contest.
Here are the scores after two throws.

Name	First Throw (yards)	Second Throw (yards)
Arnie Ape	6	9
Ian Iguana	6	7
Terry Toad	8	9
Mark Moose	5	4
Brittany Bear	7	8
Mary Mouse	6	6

Add the two throws for each contestant.
Write the totals on the chart.

Team Number	Name	Total Yards Thrown
1	Arnie	
1	Ian	
2	Terry	
2	Mark	
3	Brittany	
3	Mary	

Which putter had the most yards? _____

Which putter had the least yards? _____

Which two putters tied for the same number of yards?

_____ _____

Which team member had more total yards?

Team 1 _____

Team 2 _____

Team 3 _____

Field Day Fun

Solve each subtraction problem to help Robby Rabbit make it to the end of the race.

$$\begin{array}{r} 5 \\ -3 \\ \hline \end{array}$$
$$\begin{array}{r} 6 \\ -3 \\ \hline \end{array}$$
$$\begin{array}{r} 3 \\ -2 \\ \hline \end{array}$$
$$\begin{array}{r} 9 \\ -6 \\ \hline \end{array}$$
$$\begin{array}{r} 5 \\ -4 \\ \hline \end{array}$$
$$\begin{array}{r} 7 \\ -4 \\ \hline \end{array}$$

$$\begin{array}{r} 4 \\ -3 \\ \hline \end{array}$$
$$\begin{array}{r} 9 \\ -1 \\ \hline \end{array}$$
$$\begin{array}{r} 9 \\ -5 \\ \hline \end{array}$$
$$\begin{array}{r} 8 \\ -4 \\ \hline \end{array}$$

$$\begin{array}{r} 8 \\ -6 \\ \hline \end{array}$$
$$\begin{array}{r} 5 \\ -2 \\ \hline \end{array}$$
$$\begin{array}{r} 4 \\ -2 \\ \hline \end{array}$$
$$\begin{array}{r} 5 \\ -5 \\ \hline \end{array}$$

$$\begin{array}{r} 6 \\ -2 \\ \hline \end{array}$$
$$\begin{array}{r} 8 \\ -3 \\ \hline \end{array}$$
$$\begin{array}{r} 8 \\ -5 \\ \hline \end{array}$$
$$\begin{array}{r} 7 \\ -2 \\ \hline \end{array}$$

$$\begin{array}{r} 3 \\ -3 \\ \hline \end{array}$$
$$\begin{array}{r} 8 \\ -2 \\ \hline \end{array}$$
$$\begin{array}{r} 6 \\ -4 \\ \hline \end{array}$$
$$\begin{array}{r} 5 \\ -0 \\ \hline \end{array}$$
$$\begin{array}{r} 7 \\ -3 \\ \hline \end{array}$$
$$\begin{array}{r} 9 \\ -7 \\ \hline \end{array}$$

Finish

Field Day Fun

Running Out of Time

3:00   3:30

Write the times for each event.

100-Yard Dash	Shot Put	High Jump	The Mile Run
: _____	: _____	: _____	: _____

220-Yard Dash	Broad Jump	Hurdles	Relay Race
: _____	: _____	: _____	: _____

Draw the hands on the clocks.

50-Yard Dash	One-Mile Walk	Pole Vault	Triple Jump

9:00	11:00	5:30	12:30

Telling Time to the Hour

Race Through the Maze

Follow the signs to get through the maze.

This way →

Sharp turn

6	5	4	9	7	9
+ 7	+ 6	+ 7	+ 5	+ 5	+ 3

9	6	8	8	4	8
+ 6	+ 9	+ 8	+ 4	+ 8	+ 5

Hard left

← **Back this way**

Head for the tree

9	2	8	7	9	6
+ 9	+ 8	+ 3	+ 7	+ 7	+ 6

Last turn

You've made it out!

7	6	9	8	6	9
+ 6	+ 5	+ 4	+ 7	+ 8	+ 8

Addition Facts to 18

Field Day Fun

Randy Raccoon's Personal Best

 Randy ran a mile every day for a week. He kept track of his times.

Day 1—16 minutes
Day 2—15 minutes, 45 seconds
Day 3—15 minutes, 45 seconds
Day 4—15 minutes, 30 seconds
Day 5—15 minutes, 45 seconds
Day 6—15 minutes, 15 seconds
Day 7—15 minutes

Show his times on the graph.

Times

	1	2	3	4	5	6	7
16 minutes							
15 minutes, 45 seconds							
15 minutes, 30 seconds							
15 minutes, 15 seconds							
15 minutes							

Days

Read the graph to answer the questions.

On which day did he have the best time? _____

On which day did he have the worst time? _____

On which three days did he have the same time?

_____   _____   _____

The Winning Path

Dudley Dog needs help to find the finish line. Color all the squares with the same answer as Dudley's number.

12 − 7	16 − 7	13 − 5	14 − 7	17 − 8	15 − 9
13 − 8	11 − 6	14 − 9	10 − 5	13 − 9	12 − 9
14 − 5	12 − 5	16 − 9	11 − 6	12 − 7	14 − 9
18 − 9	11 − 8	13 − 7	17 − 9	16 − 8	13 − 8

Subtraction Facts to 18

Field Day Fun

All the Way to the End

Fill in the missing numbers to run the race.

Start

40	69	97	111	357
41	70	98	112	358
42	71	99	☐	359
☐	72	100	☐	☐
☐	73	☐	115	☐
45	☐	102	116	☐
46	☐	☐	☐	☐
47	76	104	118	364
48	77	105	☐	365
☐	☐	106	☐	☐
50	☐	☐	121	☐
51	80	108	122	368
52	81	☐	123	369
☐	☐	☐	124	370
☐	☐	111	☐	371

Finish

Counting to Hundreds

Field Day Fun

Ball Toss

Each contestant tossed a ball two times. Write the equation.

1 2 3 4 5 6 7 8 9 10 11 12 13 14 15 16 17 18 →

$$4 + 7 = 11$$

1 2 3 4 5 6 7 8 9 10 11 12 13 14 15 16 17 18 →

$$6 + \boxed{} = 13$$

1 2 3 4 5 6 7 8 9 10 11 12 13 14 15 16 17 18 →

$$\boxed{} + \boxed{} = 14$$

1 2 3 4 5 6 7 8 9 10 11 12 13 14 15 16 17 18 →

$$3 + \boxed{} = 15$$

1 2 3 4 5 6 7 8 9 10 11 12 13 14 15 16 17 18 →

$$\boxed{} + \boxed{} = \boxed{}$$

1 2 3 4 5 6 7 8 9 10 11 12 13 14 15 16 17 18 →

$$\boxed{} + \boxed{} = \boxed{}$$

Field Day Fun

Writing Number Sentences

The Finish Line

The same six contestants had a race.
The times of the race are given on the chart.

Name	Time on Stopwatch
Arnie Ape	9 minutes
Ian Iguana	8 minutes
Terry Toad	7 minutes
Mark Moose	4 minutes
Brittany Bear	6 minutes
Mary Mouse	5 minutes

Answer the questions.

Who won the race? _____

Who came in last? _____

Who came in second? _____

Who finished one minute before Ian? _____

Who finished four minutes after Mary? _____

How many minutes faster was Mark than Mary? _____

Solving Word Problems; Reading a Table; Number Facts to 18 ©2001 by Evan-Moor Corp. • Math Practice at Home • EMC 4517

Know Which Race You're In

Robbie Rabbit entered every running event.

After you solve the problems, color all the boxes in which the answers are 9 or 14 to see how many races Robbie won.

9 + 9	8 + 6	7 + 6	5 + 9	14 − 7	12 − 8
8 + 5	18 − 9	15 − 7	7 + 7	16 − 8	6 + 6
8 + 8	13 − 4	15 − 6	16 − 7	17 − 8	9 + 7
17 − 9	5 + 7	7 + 8	9 + 5	16 − 9	15 − 9
18 − 8	11 − 8	15 − 8	12 − 3	16 − 8	12 − 9

Robbie won _____ races.

©2001 by Evan-Moor Corp. • Math Practice at Home • EMC 4517

Addition and Subtraction Facts to 18

The Winner's Stand

Who got which ribbon for these Field Day events?
Read the charts. Write the names on the winners' stands.

Long-Distance Run

Jose Javelina–5 minutes, 6 seconds
Jamal Jaguar–4 minutes, 58 seconds
Josh Jackrabbit–6 minutes

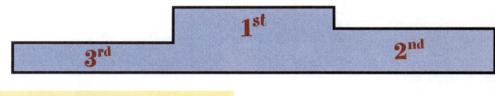

Long Jump

Hilary Hog–4 feet, 9 inches
Sarah Skunk–4 feet, 3 inches
Sang Sheep–4 feet, 11 inches
Taneka Tiger–4 feet, 10 inches

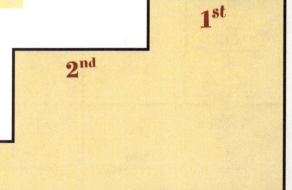

Hurdles

Sid Snake–1 minute, 3 seconds
Maya Martin–45 seconds
Carl Cricket–47 seconds
Fay Frog–1 minute, 12 seconds
Tim Tapir–59 seconds

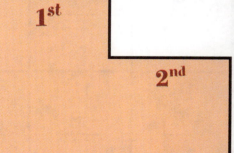

Ordinal Numbers

Field Day Fun

What's in the Shopping Cart?

When you add three or more numbers, it's easier to add pairs of numbers first.

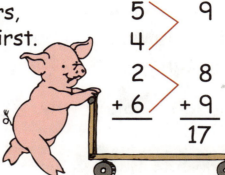

$$
\begin{array}{r}
5 \\
4 \\
2 \\
+ 6 \\
\end{array}
\quad
\begin{array}{r}
9 \\
\\
8 \\
+ 9 \\
\hline
17 \\
\end{array}
$$

Add.

$$
\begin{array}{r}
2 \\
4 \\
2 \\
+ 3 \\
\end{array}
\; + \;
\begin{array}{c}
\square \\
\\
\square \\
\hline
11 \\
\end{array}
\qquad
\begin{array}{r}
2 \\
7 \\
2 \\
+ 5 \\
\end{array}
\; + \;
\begin{array}{c}
\square \\
\\
\square \\
\hline
16 \\
\end{array}
\qquad
\begin{array}{r}
1 \\
6 \\
3 \\
+ 2 \\
\end{array}
\; + \;
\begin{array}{c}
\square \\
\\
\square \\
\hline
12 \\
\end{array}
$$

$$
\begin{array}{r}
2 \\
7 \\
7 \\
+ 3 \\
\end{array}
\; + \;
\begin{array}{c}
\square \\
\\
\square \\
\hline
\square \\
\end{array}
\qquad
\begin{array}{r}
6 \\
2 \\
2 \\
+ 6 \\
\end{array}
\; + \;
\begin{array}{c}
\square \\
\\
\square \\
\hline
\square \\
\end{array}
\qquad
\begin{array}{r}
5 \\
4 \\
3 \\
+ 3 \\
\end{array}
\; + \;
\begin{array}{c}
\square \\
\\
\square \\
\hline
\square \\
\end{array}
$$

$$
\begin{array}{r}
6 \\
1 \\
3 \\
+ 3 \\
\end{array}
\; + \;
\begin{array}{c}
\square \\
\\
\square \\
\hline
\square \\
\end{array}
\qquad
\begin{array}{r}
4 \\
4 \\
2 \\
+ 2 \\
\end{array}
\; + \;
\begin{array}{c}
\square \\
\\
\square \\
\hline
\square \\
\end{array}
\qquad
\begin{array}{r}
3 \\
4 \\
4 \\
+ 3 \\
\end{array}
\; + \;
\begin{array}{c}
\square \\
\\
\square \\
\hline
\square \\
\end{array}
$$

At the Market

Enough Money?

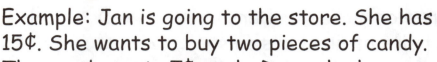

Example: Jan is going to the store. She has 15¢. She wants to buy two pieces of candy. The candy costs 7¢ each. Does she have enough money?

__yes__ Show why. _7 + 7 = 14; 14 is less than 15_

Ryan has 18¢. He wants to buy three cookies. Each cookie costs 6¢. Does he have enough money?

_____ Show why. _____

Crystal has 14¢. She wants to buy 4 gumballs. Each gumball costs 4¢. Does she have enough money?

_____ Show why. _____

Chris wants to buy 2 packs of baseball cards. Each pack costs 10¢. He only has 18¢. How much more money does he need?

_____ Show why. _____

John wants to buy 4 jawbreakers. He has 10¢. Each jawbreaker costs 3¢. How much more money does he need?

_____ Show why. _____

Jill wants to buy 5 suckers. Each sucker costs 5¢. She has a quarter. Does she have enough money?

_____ Show why. _____

How Many Groceries?

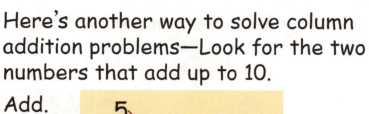

Here's another way to solve column addition problems—Look for the two numbers that add up to 10.

Add.

```
  5
  4   10
  2    4   10
+ 5  + 2  + 6
          16
```

4	4	4	3
4	7	4	7
6	2	2	3
+ 2	+ 3	+ 6	+ 3

2	2	5	1
5	1	1	5
3	1	9	1
+ 5	+ 8	+ 2	+ 5

6	7	8	5
5	7	6	4
1	3	2	4
+ 4	+ 3	+ 2	+ 5

At the Market

Column Addition

What Does It Weigh?

Match each numeral to the number word.

 4 pounds •   • twelve

 14 ounces •   • twenty-eight

 12 ounces •   • seven

 5 pounds •   • forty-nine

 28 ounces •   • four

 7 pounds •   • eighteen

 18 pounds •   • five

 49 ounces •   • fourteen

Number Words

At the Market

Fruitful Practice

Solve the problems.
Match each problem with the correct number.

```
  7          9
  1          4
  5          4
+ 3        + 1
```

```
             6
             2
             6
           + 3

     5
     7
  4  5
  6 + 4
  2
  6
+ 4
```

```
             2
             4
             2
             3
           + 1
  1
  3
  4    4
  2    6
  3    6
+ 1  + 4
```

18

21

17

14

22

20

16

12

At the Market

• Math Practice at Home • EMC 4517

Money Counts

How much money is in each set of coins?

= _____ ¢

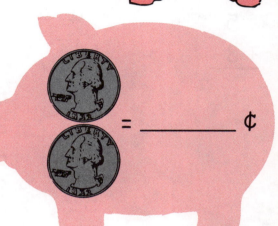

= _____ ¢

= _____ ¢

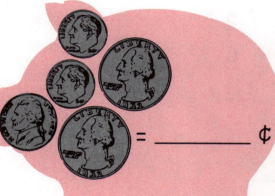

= _____ ¢

= _____ ¢

Counting Coins to 75¢

©2001 by Evan-Moor Corp. • Math Practice at Home • EMC 4517

At the Market

Percy's Purchases

Percy needs to buy
60 ounces of peanuts.
Each bag of peanuts
holds 10 ounces. How many
bags should he buy?

___6___ bags of peanuts

Show why.
10
10
10
10
10
+ 10
___

Percy needs to buy 40 ounces
of beans. Each bag holds 10 ounces.
How many bags should he buy?

_____ bags of beans

Show why.

Percy needs to buy 70 ounces
of sunflower seeds. Each bag holds
10 ounces. How many bags should
he buy?

_____ bags of seeds

Show why.

Percy needs to buy 80 ounces
of peanut butter. Each jar holds
20 ounces. How many jars should
he buy?

_____ jars of peanut butter

Show why.

At the Market

Lots of Apples

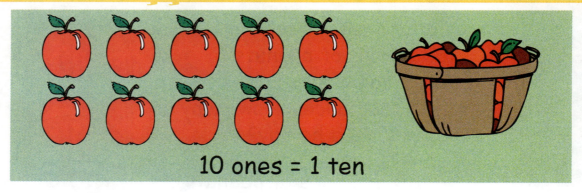

10 ones = 1 ten

Count the tens and ones. Tell how many apples.

3 baskets + 5 apples = _____

7 baskets + 2 apples = _____

8 baskets = _____

4 baskets + 8 apples = _____

1 basket + 10 apples = _____

5 baskets = _____

Place Value—Tens and Ones   ©2001 by Evan-Moor Corp. • Math Practice at Home • EMC 4517

At the Market

Farmer Jones's Roadside Stand

Farmer Jones uses a pie graph to record the fruits and vegetables he sells each day at his roadside stand.

Here is his graph for last Thursday. Read the graph. Answer the questions.

apple =

carrot =

corn =

watermelon =

squash =

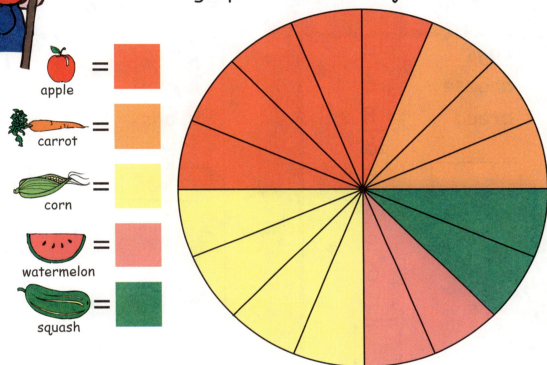

1. How many carrots were sold? _____

2. Which food sold the most? _____

3. How many more ears of corn than squash were sold? _____

4. Which food was $\frac{1}{4}$ of the total amount sold on Thursday? _____

At the Market

Check It Out!

Add the items at the check-out counter.
Then use your cents-off coupon.

9¢   8¢   4¢   5¢   6¢   5¢

eggs	4
cheese	6
bread	+ 8
	18
5¢ off	- 5
	13¢

beans	9
cheese	6
eggs	+ 4
	☐
9¢ off	- 9
	☐ ¢

popcorn	
cupcake	
eggs	+
	☐
4¢ off	-
	☐ ¢

bread	
eggs	
beans	+
	☐
7¢ off	-
	☐ ¢

cupcake	
beans	
cheese	+
	☐
3¢ off	-
	☐ ¢

Adding and Subtracting Money

Picking a Peck of Peppers

Patty Pig picks peppers to sell at the Peppy Boys Market. She uses tally marks to keep track of the peppers she picks. Help Patty track her peppers.

丗|| = 5

Week One	Tally	How Many?
Monday	IIII	4
Tuesday	丗 IIII	_____
Wednesday	丗 丗	_____
Thursday	丗 II	_____
Friday	丗 I	_____

Week Two	Tally	How Many?
Monday	丗 丗 I	_____
Tuesday	丗 II	_____
Wednesday	丗 丗 丗	_____
Thursday	丗 II	_____
Friday	丗 丗 丗 II	_____

Patty earns 1¢ for each pepper she picks.

How much did she earn in Week One? _____

In which week did she earn more money? _____

How much more? _____

©2001 by Evan-Moor Corp. • Math Practice at Home • EMC 4517   Using Tally Marks; Solving Word Problems

At the Market

How Long Is That Zucchini?

There are zucchinis of all sizes in the squash bin. Measure them.

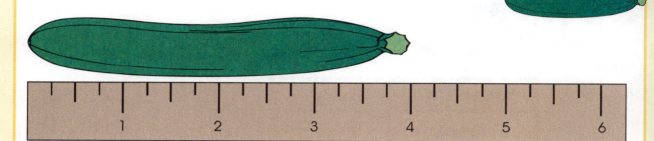

_____ inches

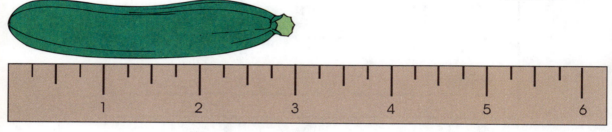

_____ inches

_____ inches

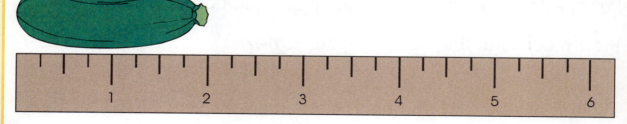

_____ inches

_____ inches

Measurement to the Nearest Inch

©2001 by Evan-Moor Corp. • Math Practice at Home • EMC 4517

At the Market

Add or subtract.

5	8	9	7	6	7	3	1
+4	+6	+0	+9	+6	+8	6	9
						5	3
						+5	+3

14	10	13	14	15	18
−9	−8	−4	−7	−8	−9

What is the time?

___ : ___   ___ : ___

How much money?

 = _____¢

What's missing?

98 99 ☐ ☐ 102 ☐

☐ ☐ 361 ☐ ☐

Match.

𝍸𝍸𝍸𝍸II •   • 16

twenty-seven •   • 19

sixteen •   • 12

𝍸𝍸𝍸𝍸𝍸𝍸IIII •   • 27

How long?

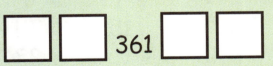

2 inches   8 inches   4 inches

Sally bought a banana for 6¢, an orange for 4¢, and an apple for 8¢. How much did she spend? _____

I Can Do It!

What's Cooking?

When you add 2-digit numbers, be sure to add the **ones** column first.

Find all the answers that have 9 in the **ones** place. Write the letters of those problems in order on the blank lines. Then you will know what's cooking!

tens	ones
1	4
+2	3
3	7

a
21
+ 5

j
11
+ 7

m
23
+ 12

d
33
+ 45

s
35
+ 14

r
21
+ 26

g
30
+ 8

h
52
+ 14

t
16
+ 23

b
63
+ 15

v
55
+ 12

l
32
+ 26

c
91
+ 3

n
44
+ 44

u
62
+ 24

p
77
+ 21

y
63
+ 33

f
80
+ 11

e
21
+ 48

i
15
+ 11

o
74
+ 23

k
34
+ 32

w
22
+ 37

x
64
+ 20

q
24
+ 71

z
42
+ 35

___ ___ ___ ___ ___

Two–Digit Addition Without Regrouping

Surprise, Surprise!

Chef Louis has created a wonderful surprise for dessert. Shade each square where the answer has 6 in the **tens** place. This will tell you the first letter of the surprise. Then circle the picture of the surprise desert.

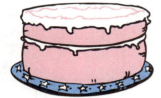  

69 − 36	79 − 15	87 − 23	96 − 33	88 − 24	47 − 12
77 − 52	95 − 35	39 − 14	87 − 54	68 − 6	90 − 60
99 − 86	87 − 25	78 − 15	74 − 12	99 − 35	72 − 41
96 − 71	67 − 7	66 − 33	68 − 55	97 − 63	88 − 64
75 − 62	82 − 20	98 − 24	99 − 4	40 − 20	56 − 25
68 − 27	77 − 11	83 − 42	80 − 40	59 − 49	58 − 17

In the Kitchen

Cookies, Cookies, and More Cookies

Help Baker Bob know how many cookies he can make. Fill in the table.

One Batch	Two Batches	Three Batches	Four Batches
20			
30			120
40		120	
12			
21			

It takes one-half hour to bake a big tray of cookies. Write the time each tray of cookies will be done.

_1:30_

_____ : _____

_____ : _____

_____ : _____

_____ : _____

_____ : _____

Addition Without Regrouping; Telling Time to the Half Hour ©2001 by Evan-Moor Corp. • Math Practice at Home • EMC 4517

Busy Bakers

Write each problem and then solve it.

Ann's cookie recipe makes 12 cookies.
If she makes a double batch,
how many cookies will she have?

_____ cookies

Fred made two cookies for each
of his kids. He has three kids.
How many cookies did Fred make?

_____ cookies

Bob had 10 eggs.
He used 4 eggs to make bread.
He used 2 eggs to make cookies.
How many eggs does he have left?

_____ eggs

Jill baked this cake.
Show how she cut the cake
for eight people. Make each
piece the same size.

Jerry bought 3 dozen donuts.
How many donuts does he have?
(hint: 1 dozen = 12)

_____ donuts

In the Kitchen

Measure It!

Measure the milk. Color to show the right amount.

1½ cups

1¼ cups

¾ cup

2¾ cups

Measure the butter. Color to show the right amount.

1½ sticks

¾ stick

2⅓ sticks

1¼ sticks

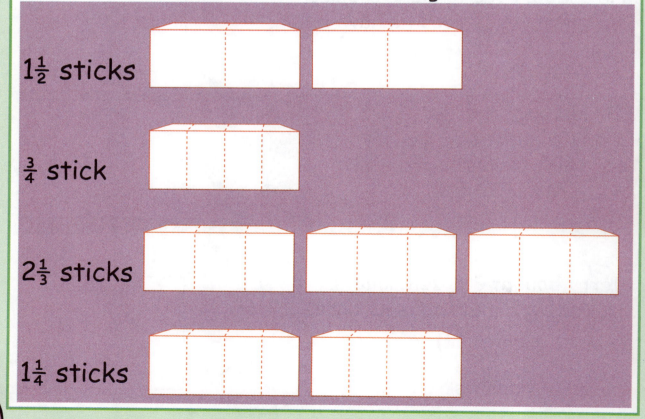

In the Kitchen

Fractions; Measurement

Snack Time

Healthy Hillary is looking for a snack. She wants to keep her snack under 250 calories because she will have a big dinner later.

Add up the calories in each snack. Then circle each snack that Hillary might choose.

200 calories   10 calories

20 calories   104 calories

80 calories   100 calories

Yum!

(Apple & Pretzel)

$$\begin{array}{r} 80 \\ + 20 \\ \hline 100 \end{array} \text{ calories}$$

Hot Dog & Ice Cream

Peanut Butter & Celery

Hot Dog & Apple

Ice Cream, Apple, & Celery

In the Kitchen

Adding Two- and Three-Digit Numbers Without Regrouping

Pizza Fractions

$\frac{1}{2}$ = one of 2 equal parts

$\frac{1}{3}$ = one of 3 equal parts

$\frac{1}{4}$ = one of 4 equal parts

$\frac{1}{8}$ = one of 8 equal parts

Color to show the fraction.

$\frac{1}{2}$

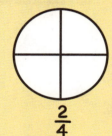

$\frac{2}{4}$

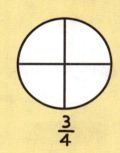

$\frac{3}{4}$

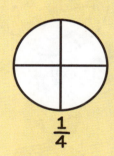

$\frac{1}{4}$

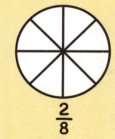

$\frac{2}{8}$

$\frac{4}{8}$

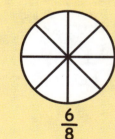

$\frac{6}{8}$

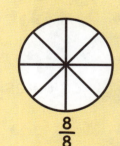

$\frac{8}{8}$

$\frac{1}{3}$

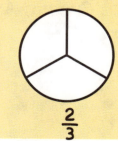

$\frac{2}{3}$

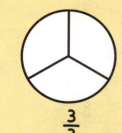

$\frac{3}{3}$

In the Kitchen

Fractions

What's the Secret Ingredient?

Add.

K	A	O	I	N	F
155	72	103	362	560	200
+ 21	+ 27	+ 95	+ 17	+ 15	+ 76

Y	A	N	D	C	D
904	303	42	88	543	43
+ 13	+ 55	+ 33	+ 10	+ 33	+ 21

I	T	O	N	G	I
176	404	654	711	100	155
+ 10	+ 51	+ 13	+ 32	+ 99	+ 11

T	W	O	U	R	S
77	17	111	234	19	30
+ 10	+ 42	+ 23	+ 55	+ 20	+ 49

Write the letter that goes with each answer to find the secret ingredient.

__ __ __ __ __ __ __ __ __ __ __

176 75 198 59 379 575 199   917 134 289 39

__ __ __ __ __ __ __ __ __ __ __ __ __

99 98 64 186 455 166 667 743   276 358 576 87 79

In the Kitchen

Family Favorites

Alex surveyed his family to find out what foods were their favorites. He marked each food that a person liked.

	Pizza	Hamburger	Taco	Stir Fry	Hot Dog
Mom	X			X	
Dad	X	X	X		X
Cleo	X	X			
Alex	X	X	X	X	X
Malcolm	X		X	X	

Use the chart to complete this graph.

Number of People

6					
5					
4					
3					
2					
1					

Pizza   Hamburger   Taco   Stir Fry   Hot Dog

Answer these questions about the graph.

What food does everyone like? _____

What food do the fewest people like? _____

Which foods have the same number of votes?

_____ _____ _____

Which of the foods on the graph is your favorite?

_____

Reading and Creating a Graph

In the Kitchen

Cookie Fractions

$\frac{1}{2}$ < $\frac{3}{4}$

Color the correct number of cookies.
Use >, <, or = to compare the amounts.

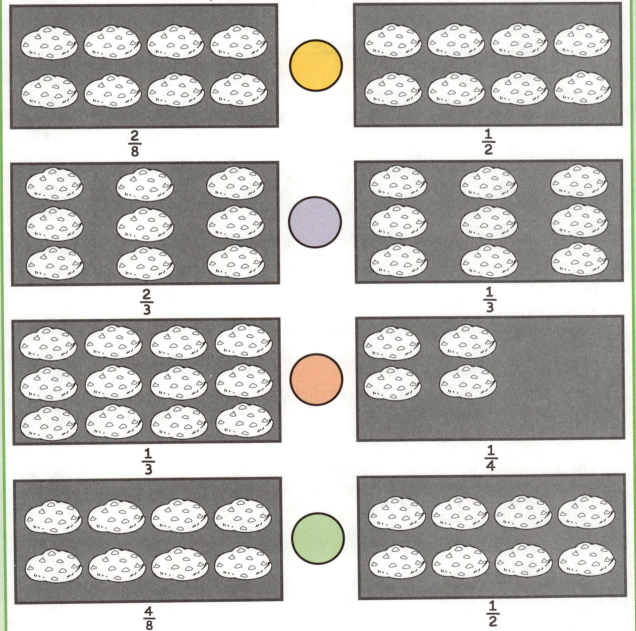

$\frac{2}{8}$ ◯ $\frac{1}{2}$

$\frac{2}{3}$ ◯ $\frac{1}{3}$

$\frac{1}{3}$ ◯ $\frac{1}{4}$

$\frac{4}{8}$ ◯ $\frac{1}{2}$

In the Kitchen

What Did You Eat?

Your meal cost $8.00. What did you eat?

Menu

Hot Dog	$4.00	Hamburger	$5.00
Sandwich	$7.00	Chips	$1.00

Show your work.

$$\begin{array}{r} \$7.00 \\ + \$1.00 \\ \hline \$8.00 \end{array}$$

_____ sandwich and chips _____

Your meal cost $10.00. What did you eat?

Menu

Pizza	$7.00	Drink	$2.00
Salad	$3.00	Ice Cream	$4.00

Show your work.

_____

Your meal cost $12.00. What did you eat?

Menu

Taco	$2.00	Burrito	$3.00
Corn Chips	$1.00	Nachos	$7.00

Show your work.

_____

In the Kitchen

Cover the Table

Make a colorful table cover.

Choose 3 colors.

Color each row of squares in the pattern given.

Row 1—ABC   Row 4—AABC

Row 2—ABBA   Row 5—ABBC

Row 3—ABCC

1

2

3

4

5

In the Kitchen

Just Ducky!

Why do ducks have big bills?

Subtract.

24 − 4 **20**	45 − 11	98 − 37	35 − 10	64 − 54	76 − 44

88 − 44	51 − 21	17 − 9	12 − 6	16 − 9	14 − 5

Circle the word beside each answer you find below. You will not find all the answers. Read the circled words from top to bottom.

1 Ducks	20 (Because)	4 They	33 The
0 run	3 for	18 the	9 they
6 buy	21 go	5 have	19 big
2 and	10 a	40 of	22 to
14 hot	15 fun	34 lot	38 done

Subtraction Facts; 2-Digit Subtraction

Fun and Games

If you draw a line through the middle of something and both sides are the same, the object is symmetrical.

Draw to make the pictures symmetrical.

Symmetry

Fun and Games

Can You Believe Your Eyes?

Color answers that **end** in:

0 green	2 purple	4 red
1 blue	3 violet	5 orange

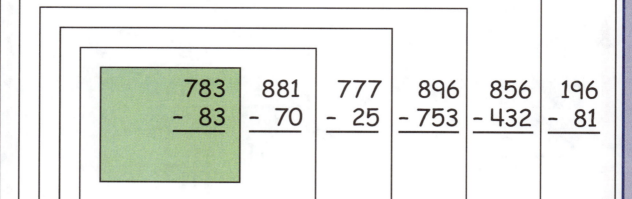

783	881	777	896	856	196
− 83	− 70	− 25	− 753	− 432	− 81

Three-Digit Subtraction Without Regrouping

Which Ride?

Lizzie, Sam, and Missy each took a different path at the amusement park.

Lizzie took the counting-by-tens path.
Sam took the counting-by-fives path.
Missy took the counting-by-twos path.

Color the 10s path red. Color the 5s path blue. Color the 2s path green.

Write each name beside the ride where his or her path led.

Missy ↓   Sam ↓   Lizzie ↓

2	9	11	25	5	10	18	10	7	23
4	6	8	27	29	15	19	20	9	29
21	25	10	30	25	20	21	30	11	30
23	27	12	14	30	35	40	40	13	120
22	20	18	16	31	32	45	50	17	110
24	33	13	33	60	55	50	60	18	100
29	3	17	3	65	13	25	70	80	90

Ferris wheel _____

bumper cars _____

merry-go-round _____

Fun and Games

Counting by 2s, 5s, and 10s

Basketball Pointers

Write each problem. Then solve it.

The Bulldogs basketball team ended the game with 76 points. The Tigers had 66 points. By how many points did the Bulldogs win?

_____

The Lions had 46 points at the end of the game. They made 24 points in the first half. How many points did they make in the second half?

_____

The Bulldogs played nine players in the first half and eight different players in the second half. How many Bulldogs played in the game?

_____

The Tigers' score was 24. That score was 64 points less than the Bulldogs' score. What was the Bulldogs' score?

_____

The Bulldogs bought three new basketballs for the game. Each ball cost $20.00. How much did the team spend?

_____

The clock showed 55 seconds left in the game. The next play took 32 seconds. How many seconds were left in the game?

_____

Fun and Games

Cowboy Dan is fixin' to lasso up some money to buy some new duds.

Circle the amount of money needed to buy each thing.

A Goofy Riddle

What can you wear that everyone will like?

A – 24	E – 22	G – 53	R – 45
B – 35	I – 12	N – 16	T – 17

$$87 - 63 = \boxed{}$$

$$68 - 15 = \boxed{} \quad 89 - 44 = \boxed{} \quad 59 - 37 = \boxed{} \quad 78 - 54 = \boxed{} \quad 78 - 61 = \boxed{}$$

_____

$$69 - 34 = \boxed{} \quad 74 - 62 = \boxed{} \quad 99 - 46 = \boxed{} \qquad 87 - 34 = \boxed{} \quad 56 - 11 = \boxed{} \quad 48 - 36 = \boxed{} \quad 99 - 83 = \boxed{}$$

___   ___   ___   ___   ___   ___   ___

Draw the answer here.

Two-Digit Subtraction Without Regrouping

Fun and Games

Explorer Ed must cross a river full of hungry crocodiles. He could jump from rock to rock.
But what if one of those rocks is really a crocodile?

Luckily, Ed knows that the **even-numbered** answers are **rocks**. The odd-numbered answers are not rocks, but crocodiles.

Even numbers, counting by 2s: 2, 4, 6, 8, 10, and so on

Odd numbers: 1, 3, 5, 7, 9, 11, and so on

Solve each problem. Then color the safe route for Explorer Ed.

$14 - 6 = 8$

$15 - 8 =$

$12 - 8 =$

$6 + 6 =$

$9 + 8 =$

$10 - 6 =$

$16 - 8 =$

$9 + 7 =$

$7 + 5 =$

$8 + 7 =$

$18 - 9 =$

$14 - 8 =$

$7 + 5 =$

$7 + 6 =$

Fun and Games

Addition and Subtraction Facts; Odd and Even Numbers

Hit the Bull's-Eye

Play this game by yourself or with a friend.

Rules for One:	Rules for Two:
Drop a coin 2 times on the target. Add the numbers. If your score is more than 50, you win.	Take turns. Drop a coin 2 times. Add the numbers. The highest score wins.

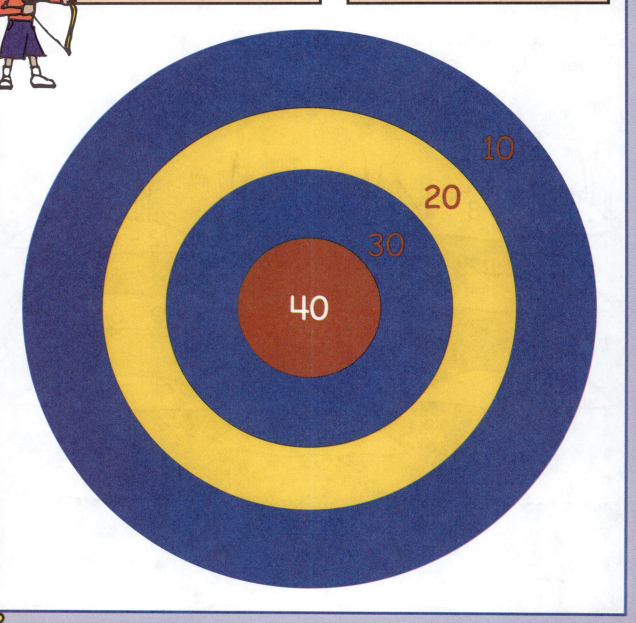

Two-Digit Addition Without Regrouping

Fun and Games

Three football players made these points: 3, 7, 21
Ron made the most points.
Mike made more points than Fred.
How many points did Fred make?

	3	7	21
Ron			X
Mike		X	
Fred	X		

<u>Fred made 3 points.</u>

Four soccer players made these goals: 0, 1, 2, 3
Joann made one goal.
Heather made twice as many goals
  as Joann.
Mandy made one more goal than
  Heather.
How many goals did Angela make?

	0	1	2	3
Heather				
Joann				
Mandy				
Angela				

_____

Three football players made these points: 6, 12, 18
John made the most points.
Gerry made half of what Bob made.
How many points did Bob make?

	6	12	18
John			
Gerry			
Bob			

_____

Five basketball players made these points: 10, 12, 12, 14, 20
Jane made the fewest points.
Debra made twice as many points
  as Jane.
Katie and Julie each made two more
  points than Jane.
How many points did Susan make?

	10	12	14	20
Katie				
Julie				
Debra				
Susan				
Jane				

_____

Fun and Games

Tick-Tock, Very Odd Clocks

When the minute hand is on the 9, it is 45 minutes past the hour.

When the minute hand is on the 3, it is 15 minutes past the hour.

8:45

7:15

Write the time shown on each clock.

___ : ___

___ : ___

___ : ___

___ : ___

___ : ___

___ : ___

___ : ___

___ : ___

___ : ___

___ : ___

___ : ___

___ : ___

50

Tell Time to the Quarter Hour

It Marks the Spot

Color the answers that **end** in **3** red.

433 − 100	404 − 300	995 − 870	556 − 401	887 − 343	345 − 12
999 − 405	275 − 252	555 − 341	756 − 752	456 − 123	779 − 505
665 − 660	777 − 543	507 − 104	567 − 234	708 − 404	567 − 222
888 − 123	386 − 222	678 − 345	914 − 801	997 − 303	668 − 663
587 − 543	789 − 456	695 − 341	446 − 132	339 − 126	554 − 110
456 − 123	854 − 330	449 − 434	568 − 63	657 − 223	828 − 525

What marks the spot? _____

©2001 by Evan-Moor Corp. • Math Practice at Home • EMC 4517

Three-Digit Subtraction Without Regrouping

51

Note: Use this assessment after your child has completed pages 28–51.

Add or subtract.

21	33	72	58	68	226
+ 17	+ 44	+ 27	− 36	− 34	+ 102

Show ¼ of the set.

What fraction is colored?

_____   _____   _____

Read the graph.

Cookies

Deb Fred Rob Bob

Who ate the most? _____

Who had two less than Rob? _____

How many did Fred eat? _____

Circle $1.42.

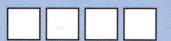

What time is it?

___ : ___   ___ : ___

Are both sides the same?

Yes   No

Circle the odd numbers.
Box the even numbers.

6	11	13	4
9	12	14	7

Count by 2s: __12__, _____, _____, _____, _____

Count by 5s: __15__, _____, _____, _____, _____

I Can Do It!

When Will It Rain?

If the **ones** place adds up to more than 9, you must **regroup**.
That means you move the **tens** to the **tens place**.
Here's how:

$$16$$
$$+\ 16$$

Add the **ones**.

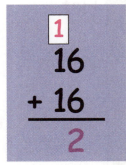

$$1$$
$$16$$
$$+\ 16$$
$$2$$

Write the ones.
Move the tens to
the tens place.

$$1$$
$$16$$
$$+\ 16$$
$$32$$

Add the **tens**.

Weather Watch

Solve the problems.

M	I	A	T
18	33	57	44
+ 8	+ 29	+ 18	+ 28

S	F	Y	U
65	29	15	77
+ 15	+ 29	+ 68	+ 13

W	O	R	D
19	38	16	54
+ 47	+ 38	+ 26	+ 19

Write the letter for each answer below to find out when it
will rain.

___ ___ ___ ___ ___ ___
58   42   62   73   75   83

•

Dressed to Go

Use the thermometer to help you decide what to wear.

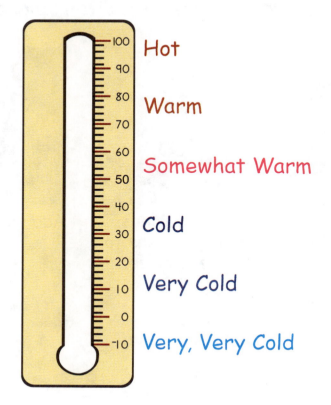

It's 10°F.

It's 40°F.

It's 65°F.

It's 100°F.

How Much Did it Snow?

Remember to add the ones first. Write the **ones** in the **ones** place; move the **tens** to the **tens** place.

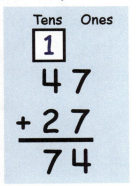

Tens	Ones
1	

```
  4 7
+ 2 7
-----
  7 4
```

```
  73
+  9
----
```

```
  57
+ 23
----
```

```
  44
+  7
----
```

```
  64
+  9
----
```

```
  74
+ 19
----
```

```
  45
+ 36
----
```

```
  28
+ 46
----
```

```
  17
+ 47
----
```

```
  39
+  8
----
```

```
  52
+ 29
----
```

```
  44
+ 16
----
```

```
  26
+ 46
----
```

Circle the largest number in the **tens** place.
That will tell you how many inches it snowed.

It snowed _____ inches.

Two-Digit Addition with Regrouping

Let it Snow!

Write the problems. Then solve them.

1

It began snowing at 2:00 in the afternoon. At 8:00 that night it stopped. How many hours did it snow?

_____

2

If it snowed 2 inches every hour, how many inches of snow were there at 8:00?

_____

3

There were 28 children at the sledding hill. There were 18 sleds. How many children did **not** have a sled?

_____

4

The sledding hill is 220 feet long. How many feet will I sled if I go down the hill three times?

_____

5

My friends and I built 3 snow people. Each snow person was decorated with 2 sticks, 1 hat, and 4 buttons. How many of each thing did we use in all?

sticks _____

hats _____

buttons _____

6

The snow made it hard to drive on the roads. The news report said that 36 cars and 17 trucks had gotten stuck in the snow. How many vehicles got stuck?

_____

Weather Watch

Count by 2s.

2 ____ 6 ____ 10

20 22 ____ 26

48 ____ 52 54 ____

70 ____ ____ 76 ____ 80

A Fahrenheit thermometer is usually marked in 2-degree units.

Read each thermometer and write the temperature.

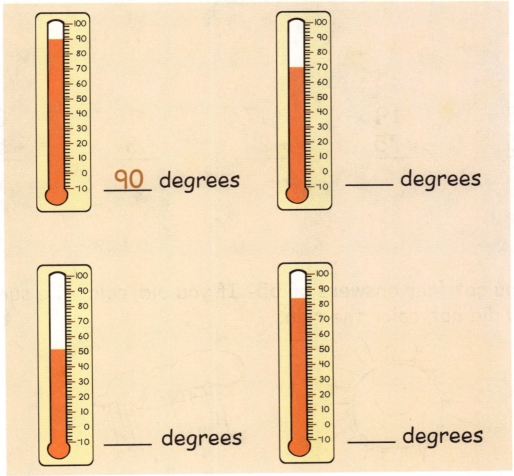

_90_ degrees

____ degrees

____ degrees

____ degrees

Counting by 2s; Reading a Thermometer

Weather Watch

Rain or Shine?

Add. Remember to add the ones first and then move any tens to the tens place.

17 + 7	15 + 9	18 + 8	14 + 9	19 + 9
17 + 38	19 + 15	19 + 53	29 + 26	36 + 19
28 + 35	19 + 75	17 + 24	18 + 37	34 + 57

Did you get four answers of 55? If you did, color the sun. If you did not, color the rain.

Two-Digit Addition with Regrouping

Foul-Weather Gear

Color to show the fractions.

1/2

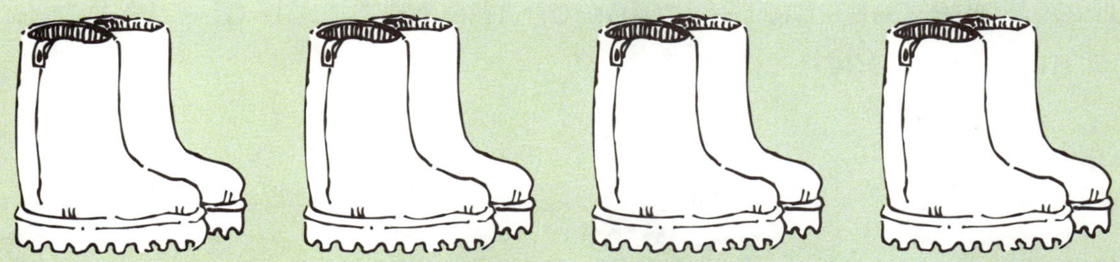

1/3

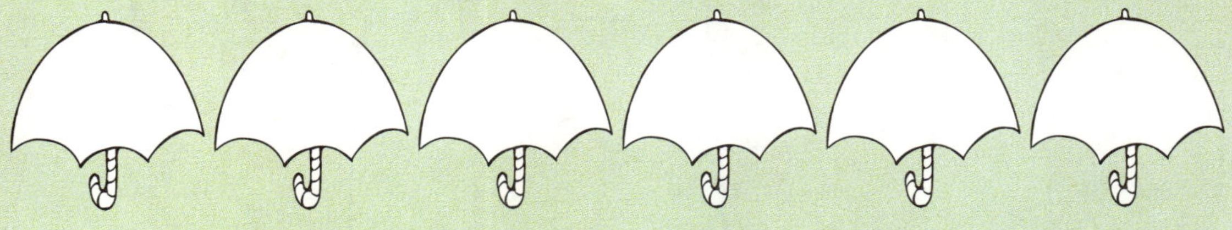

1/4

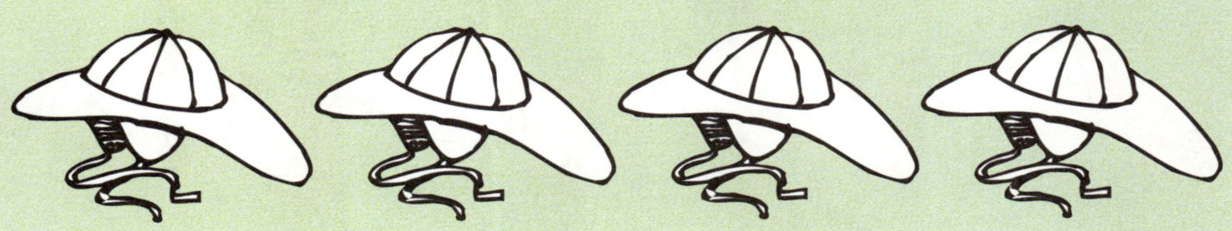

2/3

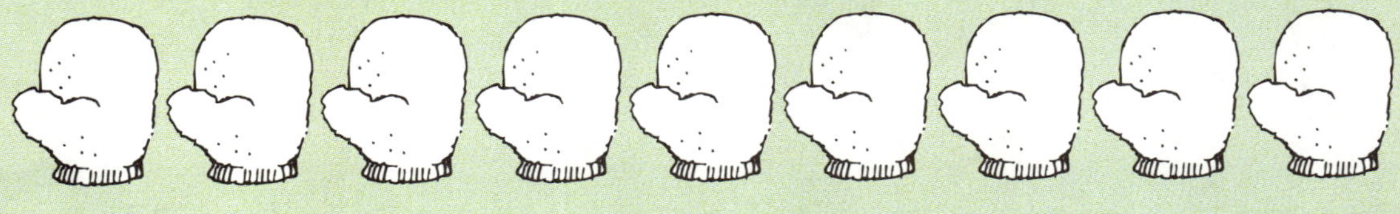

3/4

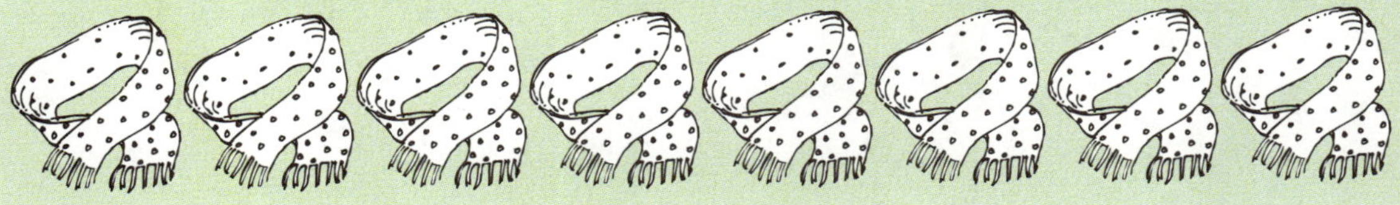

Weather Watch

How Long Are the Snowmen's Noses?

centimeters

1 2 3 4 5 6 7 8 9 10 11 12 13 14 15 16 17 18 19 20 21 22 23 24

Here are some carrots used to make noses for five snowmen. Cut out the centimeter ruler on the left side of the page and measure each carrot.

_____ cm   _____ cm   _____ cm   _____ cm   _____ cm

Measuring to the Nearest Centimeter

Drip Drop

Draw lines to match the problems with their answers.

73

$$\begin{array}{r} 26 \\ + 26 \\ \hline \end{array} \qquad \begin{array}{r} 56 \\ + 35 \\ \hline \end{array}$$

87

52

$$\begin{array}{r} 28 \\ + 45 \\ \hline \end{array} \qquad \begin{array}{r} 49 \\ + 38 \\ \hline \end{array}$$

96

91

$$\begin{array}{r} 54 \\ + 29 \\ \hline \end{array} \qquad \begin{array}{r} 68 \\ + 28 \\ \hline \end{array}$$

65

44

$$\begin{array}{r} 19 \\ + 46 \\ \hline \end{array} \qquad \begin{array}{r} 39 \\ + 39 \\ \hline \end{array}$$

78

62

$$\begin{array}{r} 15 \\ + 47 \\ \hline \end{array} \qquad \begin{array}{r} 37 \\ + 7 \\ \hline \end{array}$$

83

Weather Watch

Two-Digit Addition with Regrouping

Graphing the Temperature

This line graph shows the temperature for the first 18 days of July. Use the graph to answer the questions.

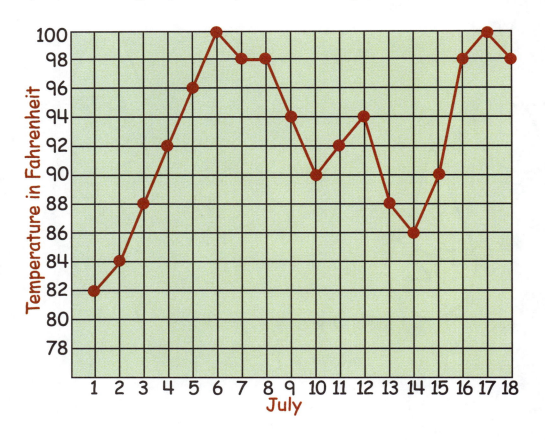

What was the temperature on the coldest day? _____

Which two days were the hottest? _____

How hot was it? _____

Starting with July 1, how many days
in a row did the temperature go up? _____

What was the temperature on July 10? _____

What was the difference between the
temperatures on July 14 and July 16? _____

Reading a Graph

Weather Watch

Some problems need regrouping. Some problems don't.
Color the sun on all the problems where you **did not** need
to regroup.

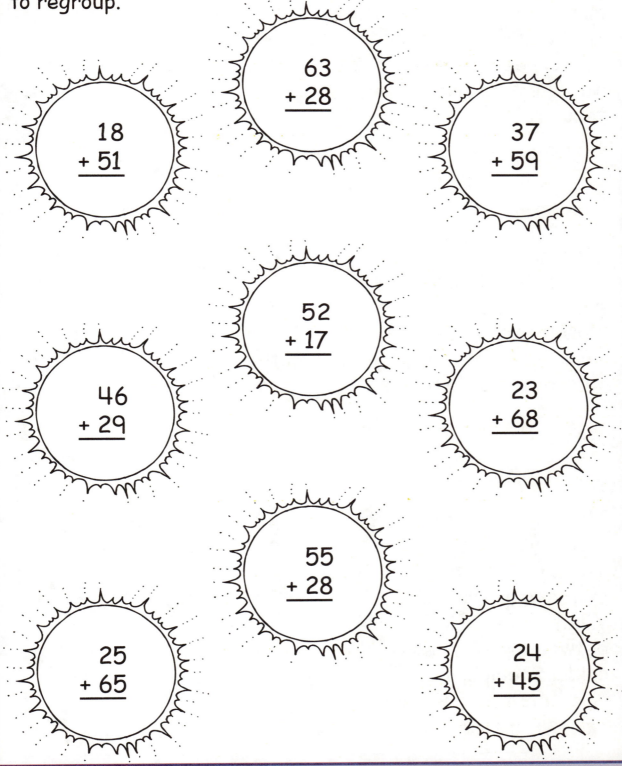

$$\begin{array}{r} 18 \\ + 51 \\ \hline \end{array}$$

$$\begin{array}{r} 63 \\ + 28 \\ \hline \end{array}$$

$$\begin{array}{r} 37 \\ + 59 \\ \hline \end{array}$$

$$\begin{array}{r} 46 \\ + 29 \\ \hline \end{array}$$

$$\begin{array}{r} 52 \\ + 17 \\ \hline \end{array}$$

$$\begin{array}{r} 23 \\ + 68 \\ \hline \end{array}$$

$$\begin{array}{r} 25 \\ + 65 \\ \hline \end{array}$$

$$\begin{array}{r} 55 \\ + 28 \\ \hline \end{array}$$

$$\begin{array}{r} 24 \\ + 45 \\ \hline \end{array}$$

Two-Digit Addition With and Without Regrouping

Weather Watch

What's the Temperature?

Write the problems. Then solve them.

The temperature this morning was 36 degrees. In the afternoon it was 27 degrees warmer. What was the afternoon temperature?

_____

In the afternoon the temperature was 65 degrees. In the evening it was 31 degrees cooler. What was the evening temperature?

_____

This morning the temperature was sixty-two degrees. Now it is nine degrees warmer. What is the temperature now?

_____

Dad says it may snow if the temperature falls to 32°F. It is 48° now. How many degrees must the temperature fall for it to snow?

_____

The hottest temperature of the year was 98°F. The coldest temperature of the year was 26°F. What was the difference between the hottest and coldest temperatures?

_____

Mom says we cannot go swimming until the temperature reaches 75°. The thermometer now reads 60°. How much does the temperature need to rise before we can go swimming?

_____

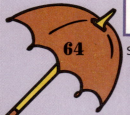

Weather Watch

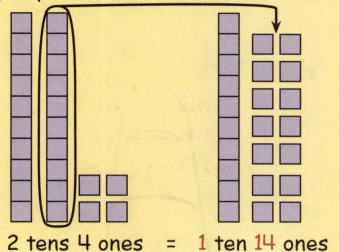

Regroup to make one less set of tens.

2 tens 4 ones = 1 ten 14 ones

6 tens 5 ones = __5__ tens __15__ ones

9 tens 2 ones = __8__ tens __12__ ones

2 tens 7 ones = ____ tens ____ ones

8 tens 6 ones = ____ tens ____ ones

5 tens 8 ones = ____ tens ____ ones

6 tens 1 ones = ____ tens ____ ones

9 tens 4 ones = ____ tens ____ ones

7 tens 0 ones = ____ tens ____ ones

Outer Space

Up, Up and Away!

Connect the dots. Start at 179.

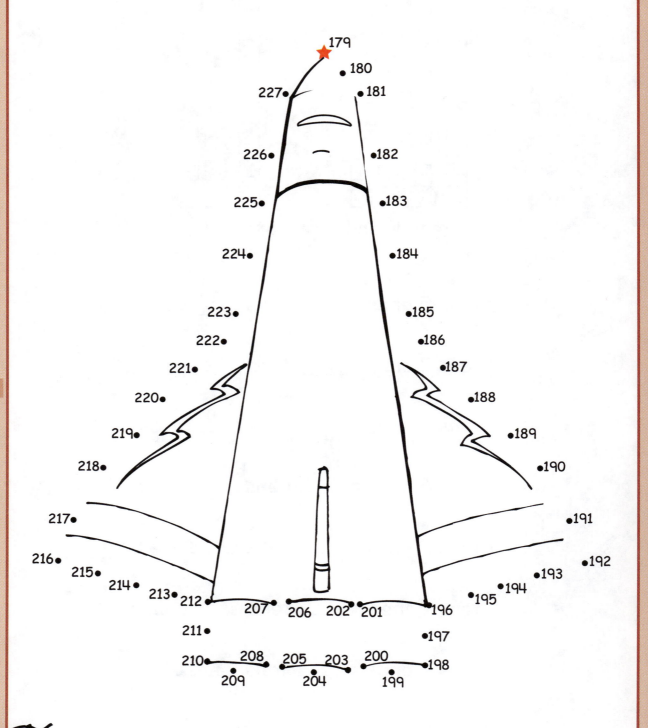

Counting by Ones

©2001 by Evan-Moor Corp. • Math Practice at Home • EMC 4517

Outer Space

Regrouping to Subtract

Draw 2 tens sticks. Regroup a ten stick. Subtract 1 unit.

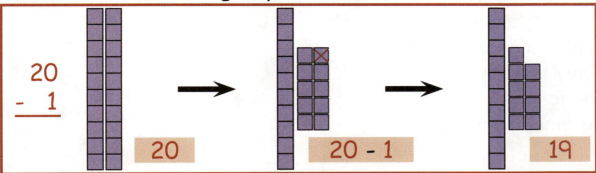

20
- 1

20   20 - 1   19

Draw 2 tens sticks. Regroup a ten stick. Subtract 7 units.

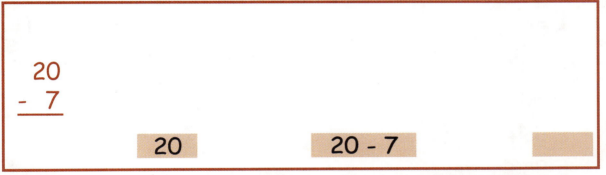

20
- 7

20   20 - 7

Draw 3 tens sticks. Regroup a ten stick. Subtract 3 units.

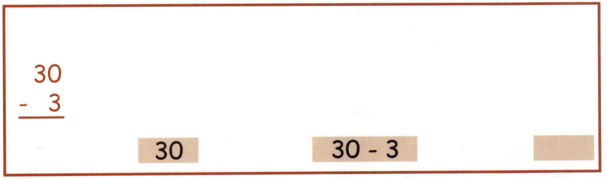

30
- 3

30   30 - 3

Draw 3 tens sticks. Regroup a ten stick. Subtract 8 units.

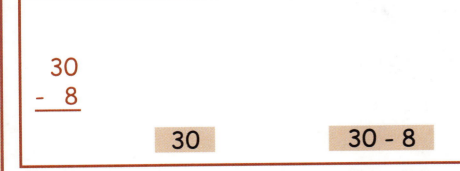

30
- 8

30   30 - 8

Two-Digit Subtraction with Regrouping

Outer Space

Moon Craters

A scientific team set out to measure some moon craters. They measured the longest distance in meters.

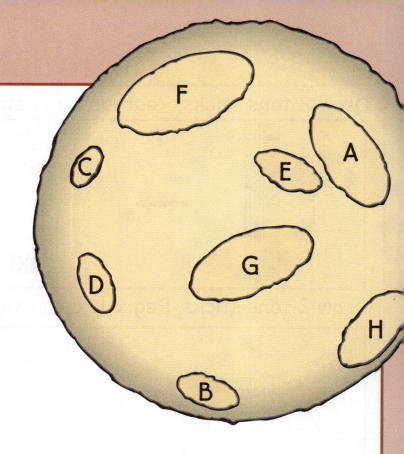

A 850 meters
B 532 meters
C 57 meters
D 300 meters
E 534 meters
F 983 meters
G 902 meters
H 775 meters

Which crater is the largest? ____

Which crater is the smallest? ____

Which craters are almost the same size? ____ ____

Which craters are longer than 780 meters? ____ ____ ____

Which crater measurement has 3 in the ones place? ____

Outer Space

In the Solar System

Write the problems. Then solve them.

Rodney Rocketman is flying his ship through the asteroid belt. Yesterday he dodged 75 asteroids. Today he dodged only 47. How many more asteroids did he dodge yesterday?

_____

The space probe reached Jupiter 38 days after it was launched. It reached Neptune 95 days after it was launched. How many more days did it take to reach Neptune?

_____

Uranus has 18 moons. Neptune has 8 moons. How many more moons does Uranus have?

_____

A year on Jupiter is about 12 Earth-years long. A year on Saturn is about 30 Earth-years long. How much longer is a year on Saturn?

_____

©2001 by Evan-Moor Corp. • Math Practice at Home • EMC 4517 Two-Digit Subtraction With and Without Regrouping

Outer Space

Subtraction with Regrouping

This is what I think when I need to regroup to subtract:

I can't take 6 away from 4, so I must regroup the tens.

Now I have 2 tens and 14 ones.

$$14 - 6 = 8$$

2 tens - 0 tens = 2 tens

tens ones
```
  2 1
  3̸ 4̸
-   6
-----
  2 8
```

```
  2 1
  3̸ 0̸        4̸ 5̸ 1        3̸ 4̸ 1        4̸ 5̸ 1        1̸ 2̸ 1
    3 0            5 1            4 3            5 0            2 8
-     3        -     8        -     5        -     7        -     9
-------        -------        -------        -------        -------
    2 7
```

```
  7 4            3 0            3 4            4 2            2 3
-   5          -   1          -   9          -   3          -   6
-----          -----          -----          -----          -----
```

```
  2 1            6 4            5 5            3 1            7 7
-   5          -   9          -   8          -   5          -   9
-----          -----          -----          -----          -----
```

Outer Space

Chores in Space

The commander of Space Station Seven posted this list of chores to be done and the times by which they need to be finished.

Match the chore with the correct clock.

Station Chores

Service escape pods   2:15 •

Put fuel in shuttle   4:05 •

Clean video screen   7:45 •

Calibrate sensors   9:50 •

Program holodeck   6:10 •

Repair replicator   11:55 •

Riddle Time

If athletes get athlete's foot, what do astronauts get?

e – 39	l – 62	t – 47
g – 78	m – 36	y – 24
h – 56	o – 89	
i – 17	s – 25	

```
  91        82        77        63
- 44      - 26      - 38      - 39
-----     -----     -----     -----
  47
  ___       ___       ___       ___
   I
```

```
            96        96        93
          - 18      - 57      - 46
          -----     -----     -----

            ___       ___       ___
```

```
  95        75        50        80        80        64
- 59      - 58      - 25      - 55      - 18      - 25
-----     -----     -----     -----     -----     -----

  ___       ___       ___       ___       ___       ___
```

```
            84        98        52
          - 37      -  9      - 13
          -----     -----     -----

            ___       ___       ___
```

Two–Digit Subtraction with Regrouping   ©2001 by Evan-Moor Corp. • Math Practice at Home • EMC 4517

Outer Space

How Many Moons?

Color the graph to show how many moons each planet has.

Mercury – no moons   Mars – 2 moons   Uranus – 18 moons

Venus – no moons   Jupiter – 16 moons   Neptune – 8 moons

Earth – 1 moon   Saturn – 18 moons   Pluto – 1 moon

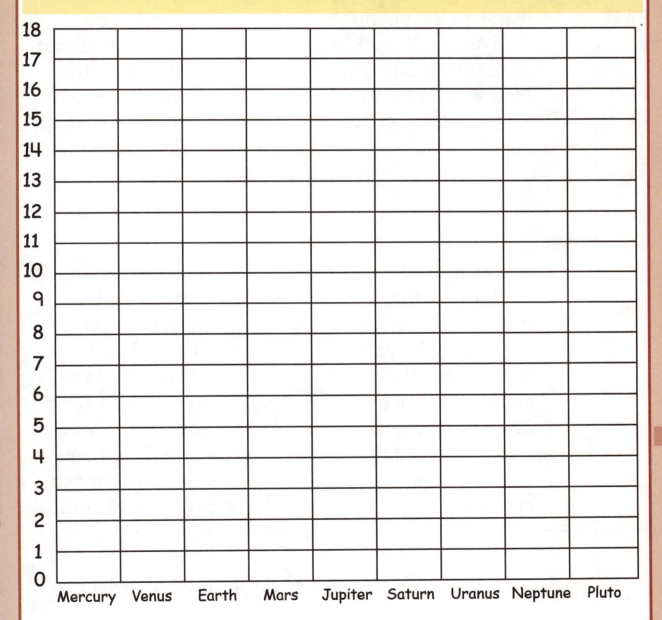

Outer Space

Creating a Graph

On the Moon

Write the problems. Then solve them.

The astronauts brought rocks back from the moon. The largest rock weighed 40 pounds. The smallest rock weighed 16 pounds. How much heavier was the largest rock?

pounds

Things weigh less on the moon than on Earth. If you weigh 54 pounds on Earth, you would weigh about 9 pounds on the moon. How much more do you weigh on Earth than on the moon?

pounds

There are many craters on the moon. One crater measured 95 yards across. Another crater measured 58 yards across. How much wider was the larger crater?

yards

You can leap much farther on the moon than on Earth. One astronaut leaped three times for a total of 63 feet. Another astronaut leaped twice and covered 49 feet. How much farther did the first astronaut leap?

feet

Two-Digit Subtraction with Regrouping

Outer Space

Larger, Smaller, Before, After

Compare the numbers. Use **>** (greater than) or **<** (less than).

7 ◯ 8   0 ◯ 1   9 ◯ 8

34 ◯ 99   41 ◯ 40   77 ◯ 66

450 ◯ 449   305 ◯ 315   942 ◯ 952

700 ◯ 800   191 ◯ 189

Write the numbers that come before and after.

_28_ 29 _30_   ____ 88 ____

____ 243 ____   ____ 460 ____

____ 622 ____   ____ 806 ____

____ 60 ____   ____ 176 ____

____ 329 ____   ____ 519 ____

____ 781 ____   ____ 987 ____

Outer Space

Space Tic-Tac-Toe

Mark an **X** on problems where you had to regroup.
Mark an **O** on problems with no regrouping.

56 - 42	37 - 14	55 - 28
62 - 31	81 - 66	84 - 21
98 - 49	96 - 34	37 - 13

Who won? _____

Two-Digit Subtraction with Regrouping

Note: Use this assessment after your child has completed pages 53–76.

Add or subtract. You may or may not need to regroup.

| 15
+ 15 | 12
+ 29 | 34
− 16 | 86
− 16 | 42
+ 17 | 41
− 39 |

Read the thermometer.

Is it hot?   ○ Yes   ○ No

What is the temperature?

_____ degrees Fahrenheit

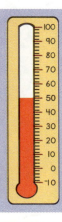

>, <, or = ?

450 ○ 350   56 ○ 52   111 ○ 113   21 ○ 21

About how many centimeters?

_____

○ 2   ○ 10   ○ 30

Write the problem. Then solve it.

Toby Turtle finished the race in 77 seconds.
Teresa Turtle finished in 68 seconds.
How much slower was Toby?

_____ seconds slower

I Can Do It!

Celebration Times

Add. Remember—if the ones are greater than 9, you must regroup and move the tens to the tens place.

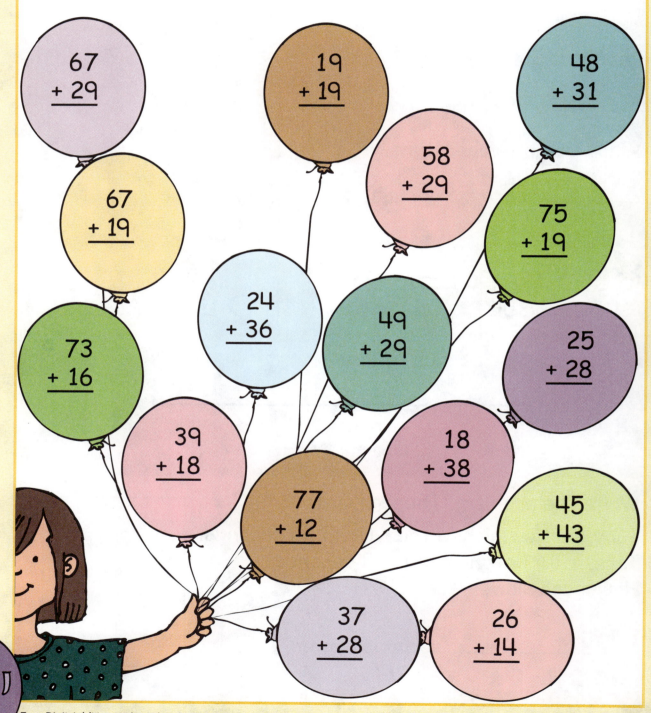

67
+ 29

19
+ 19

48
+ 31

67
+ 19

58
+ 29

75
+ 19

73
+ 16

24
+ 36

49
+ 29

25
+ 28

39
+ 18

18
+ 38

77
+ 12

45
+ 43

37
+ 28

26
+ 14

Two-Digit Addition With and Without Regrouping

The distance around something is called the perimeter.
How far is it around each shape?

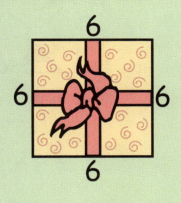

6
6   6
6

_____ 24 _____

8
4   4
8

_____

5   5
7   7
3

_____

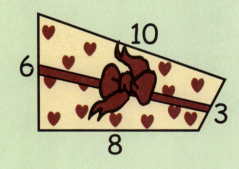

10
6
3
8

_____

4   5
4   7
2

_____

6   8
2   4
8   6

_____

Geometry—Perimeter

Subtract. Remember, if there are not enough ones to subtract, regroup the tens to make more ones.

tens ones

$$
\begin{array}{r}
2\;{}^{1} \\
\cancel{3}\;1 \\
-\quad 3 \\
\hline
2\;8
\end{array}
$$

78 − 9	57 − 26	29 − 4	36 − 9
66 − 35	56 − 28	85 − 65	47 − 25
22 − 12	93 − 37	68 − 29	52 − 16

Celebration Times

Two-Digit Subtraction With and Without Regrouping

Here are the prices of some items you might want to have at your party. Use the information to help you write and solve each problem.

balloon	party favor	party hat	noisemaker
$1.00 each	$5.00 each	$2.00 each	$3.00 each

1 How much will it cost for each person if you buy all of the party items shown?

_____

3 You've decided to have only balloons and party hats. How many friends can you invite if you have $15.00 to spend?

_____

2 You have $30.00 to spend. Can you buy all of the items for three guests?

_____

4 This is what you bought:

5

10 🎈

5 🎁

How much did you spend?

_____

Here Comes the Parade

We saw these things in the parade:

7 bands	12 clowns
4 dogs	10 floats
11 funny cars	9 bicycles
5 balloons	8 horses
3 fire trucks	

Label the graph and color in the sections to show the information above.

_____

_____

_____

_____

_____

_____

_____

bands _____

1 2 3 4 5 6 7 8 9 10 11 12

82

Making a Graph

Celebration Times

I may promise you a treasure, but watch out! I'm tricky.

P	N	E
21 + 46	56 + 43	17 + 29

R	L	C
55 + 14	39 + 16	45 + 25

E	A	U
28 + 18	48 + 28	28 + 53

H	A
67 + 26	39 + 37

Write the letter that goes with each answer.

___ ___ ___ ___ ___ ___ ___ ___ ___ ___ ___
76   55   46   67   69   46   70   93   76   81   99

The Clowns Go Marching

Write the correct ordinal number under each clown.

fourth	second	sixth
third	fifth	first

Each clown had an umbrella. Label the pattern.

A _ _ _ _ _ _ _ _ _ _ _ _ _ _ _ _ _ _

Ordinal Numbers; Patterning

Riddle Time

What do you always get a new one of, even if the old one was good?

A – 47	N – 23	W – 15
E – 56	R – 38	Y – 22

```
  67
- 20
[    ]
____
```

```
  90
- 67
[    ]
____
```

```
  82
- 26
[    ]
____
```

```
  73
- 58
[    ]
____
```

```
  90
- 68
[    ]
____
```

```
  94
- 38
[    ]
____
```

```
  58
- 11
[    ]
____
```

```
  76
- 38
[    ]
____
```

Celebration Times

Symmetrical Symbols

When you draw a line of **symmetry**, both sides are the same. Are both sides the same?

○ yes ○ no   ○ yes ○ no

○ yes ○ no   ○ yes ○ no

Draw a line of symmetry on each symbol.

A Message for You

Be careful. Some problems require regrouping; some do not.
When you are finished, color the squares with problems
where you **did not** regroup.

23 + 46	75 + 19	71 + 28	37 + 28	65 − 34
48 − 26	89 − 25	99 − 63	43 − 27	33 + 66
57 − 14	94 − 66	54 + 35	66 − 47	78 − 30

What is the secret message? _____

Celebration Times (vertical title on right side)

©2001 by Evan-Moor Corp. • Math Practice at Home • EMC 4517   Two-Digit Addition and Subtraction w/wo Regrouping

Hidden Holiday Picture

A line that connects two points is called a line segment.
We write line segments like this: $\overline{XY}$

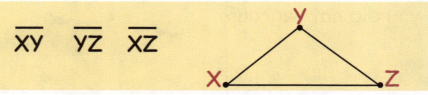

$$\overline{XY} \quad \overline{YZ} \quad \overline{XZ}$$

Draw these line segments to see what's hiding.

$$\overline{AB} \quad \overline{BG} \quad \overline{GH} \quad \overline{HA} \quad \overline{BC} \quad \overline{GF} \quad \overline{CF} \quad \overline{CD} \quad \overline{DE} \quad \overline{EF}$$

D•   •E

C•   •F

B•   •G

A•   •H

The picture you made might belong to

Geometry—Coordinate Pairs   ©2001 by Evan-Moor Corp. • Math Practice at Home • EMC 4517

Celebration Times

Congratulations! You tricked the leprechaun and now you have a pot of gold. How will you spend it?

$74 $18 $57 $85 $46

Write each problem. Then solve it.

The pot of gold has $90.00 in it. How much will you have left if you buy a baseball glove?

_____

The pot of gold has $75.00 in it. Can you buy a calculator and a doll?

_____

How much will be left if the pot of gold has $98 in it and you buy a scooter?

_____

You can buy any two of the items pictured. What would you buy? How much would it cost?

_____

Solving Word Problems

Celebration Times

How Many Legs?

How many dogs? _____2_____

How many legs on each dog? _____4_____

How many legs in all? _____8_____

How many birds? _____

How many legs on each bird? _____

How many legs in all? _____

How many insects? _____

How many legs on each insect? _____

How many legs in all? _____

How many horses? _____

How many legs on each horse? _____

How many legs in all? _____

How many birds? _____

How many legs on each bird? _____

How many legs in all? _____

Concept of Multiplication

Animals, Animals

Write each problem. Then solve it.

Timothy Turtle's favorite food is cabbage leaves. He ate 3 leaves from each of 3 cabbage plants. How many leaves did Timothy eat?

_____ leaves

Timothy is slow, but steady. He walked 1 mile every day for 5 days to get to the cabbage patch. How many miles did Timothy walk?

_____ miles

Timothy's shell has square shapes on it. There are 5 rows of squares. Each row has 5 squares. How many squares are on Timothy's shell?

_____ squares

Timothy pulls his head and legs inside his shell when he takes a nap. Timothy took 2 naps each day on Monday, Tuesday, and Wednesday. How many naps did he take?

_____ naps

Timothy joined 3 other turtles at the pond to catch flies. Each turtle caught 4 flies. How many flies were eaten in all?

_____ flies

Animals, Animals!

Home to the Hive

Connect the flowers to help Buzz Bee find his way back to the hive. You must always move to a larger number and in order.

Counting; Number Order

©2001 by Evan-Moor Corp. • Math Practice at Home • EMC 4517

How Many Spots?

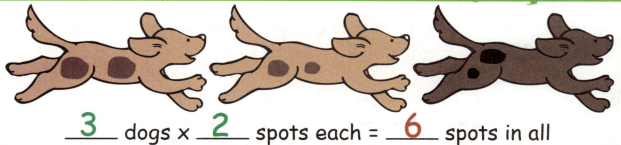

_3_ dogs x _2_ spots each = _6_ spots in all

_____ dogs x _____ spots each = _____ spots in all

_____ dogs x _____ spots each = _____ spots in all

_____ dogs x _____ spots each = _____ spots in all

Multiplication Facts

Animals, Animals

At the Roundup

Rancher Ron wants to round up some of the cattle in each herd. Color the fractions shown.

Fraction of a Group

©2001 by Evan-Moor Corp. • Math Practice at Home • EMC 4517

Counting Elephants

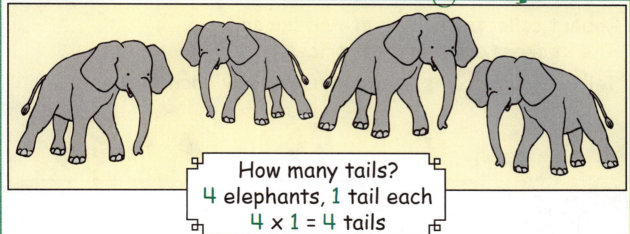

How many tails?
4 elephants, 1 tail each
4 x 1 = 4 tails

How many ears?

_____ elephants, _____ ears each

_____ x _____ = _____ ears

How many legs?

_____ elephants, _____ legs each

_____ x _____ = _____ legs

How many tusks?

_____ elephants, _____ tusks each

_____ x _____ = _____ tusks

How many trunks?

_____ elephants, _____ trunks each

_____ x _____ = _____ trunks

Multiplication Facts

Animals, Animals

Sticker Fun

Robert collects stickers of African animals.
The stickers are different prices.

Tell how many coins he would use to buy each sticker.

	penny	nickel	dime	quarter
15¢		1	1	
20¢				
32¢				
28¢				
50¢				
43¢				
65¢				
39¢				

Money—Quarter, Dime, Nickel, Penny

A Multiplication Riddle

How do you get down off a dinosaur?

0 – o	6 – n	12 – d	25 – w
2 – a	8 – e	15 – y	
3 – g	9 – k	16 – u	
4 – c	10 – f	20 – t	

$$\begin{array}{c}3\\\times 5\\\hline 15\end{array}\quad \begin{array}{c}1\\\times 0\end{array}\quad \begin{array}{c}4\\\times 4\end{array}\qquad \begin{array}{c}6\\\times 2\end{array}\quad \begin{array}{c}5\\\times 0\end{array}\quad \begin{array}{c}2\\\times 3\end{array}\quad \begin{array}{c}5\\\times 4\end{array}$$

y __ __   __ __ __ __ .

$$\begin{array}{c}5\\\times 3\end{array}\quad \begin{array}{c}3\\\times 0\end{array}\quad \begin{array}{c}8\\\times 2\end{array}\quad \begin{array}{c}3\\\times 1\end{array}\quad \begin{array}{c}2\\\times 4\end{array}\quad \begin{array}{c}4\\\times 5\end{array}\quad \begin{array}{c}3\\\times 4\end{array}\quad \begin{array}{c}0\\\times 2\end{array}\quad \begin{array}{c}5\\\times 5\end{array}\quad \begin{array}{c}6\\\times 1\end{array}$$

__ __ __ __ __ __ __ __ __ __

$$\begin{array}{c}0\\\times 4\end{array}\quad \begin{array}{c}2\\\times 5\end{array}\quad \begin{array}{c}5\\\times 2\end{array}\qquad \begin{array}{c}1\\\times 2\end{array}\qquad \begin{array}{c}4\\\times 3\end{array}\quad \begin{array}{c}4\\\times 4\end{array}\quad \begin{array}{c}2\\\times 2\end{array}\quad \begin{array}{c}3\\\times 3\end{array}$$

__ __ __   __   __ __ __ __ !

Multiplication Facts

Animals, Animals

Put Them on the Shelf

Inches

Tomika wants to put her toy animals on the shelf in order by length. Use the ruler to help Tomika measure her animals to the nearest half inch.

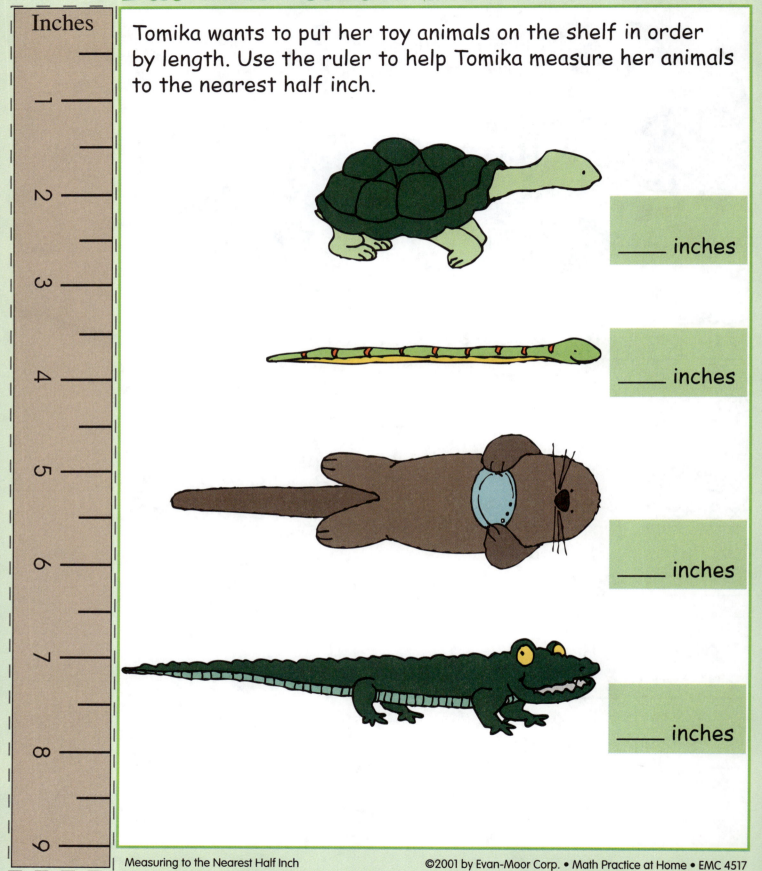

_____ inches

_____ inches

_____ inches

_____ inches

Coop Capers

Write each problem. Then solve it.

Farmer Dave has 6 hens. Each hen lays one egg a day. How many eggs will Farmer Dave collect in 3 days?

_____ eggs

The chickens sleep in cubes stacked together. There are 3 rows with 4 cubes in each row. How many chickens can take a rest at one time?

_____ chickens

Each chick eats 2 pounds of feed every week. How much feed will 8 chicks eat in a week?

_____ pounds of feed

Sometimes Farmer Dave lets the eggs hatch. Last month 3 hens hatched 5 eggs each. How many new chicks are in the coop?

_____ chicks

On Monday Farmer Dave sold 4 eggs to his neighbor. The neighbor wanted to bake a cake. She paid 5¢ an egg. How much money was Farmer Dave paid?

_____ ¢

©2001 by Evan-Moor Corp. • Math Practice at Home • EMC 4517

Solving Word Problems

99

Animals, Animals

Animal Tracks

Color each set of animal tracks to show the pattern written.

ABCC

AAB

ABAC

Animals, Animals

Help the Cows Get Home

Solve the problems. Color the answers in order to show the cows how to get home.

2	4	3	5	6	4	5	2
$\times 3$	$\times 2$	$\times 3$	$\times 1$	$\times 0$	$\times 3$	$\times 5$	$\times 2$
6							

2	5	5	6	8	4	9	0
$\times 1$	$\times 2$	$\times 3$	$\times 3$	$\times 2$	$\times 5$	$\times 2$	$\times 4$

6	2	6	20	25	16
8	5	12	4	0	9
9	5	0	12	25	6
8	4	15	9	4	3
6	12	15	10	2	8
9	16	18	12	4	10
0	2	16	20	18	0

Add or subtract.

| 75
− 27 | 46
+ 29 | 316
+ 183 | 95
− 43 | 68
− 19 | 47
+ 37 |

Fill in the blanks.

_____ groups of _____

_____ × _____ = _____

_____ groups of _____

_____ × _____ = _____

Multiply.

$4 \times 3 =$ _____ $6 \times 2 =$ _____ $5 \times 5 =$ _____ $1 \times 3 =$ _____

What is the perimeter?

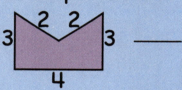
_____

Draw lines of symmetry.

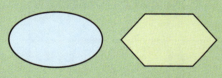

Color $\frac{1}{3}$.

Mark 63¢.

Draw a line $4\frac{1}{2}$ inches long.

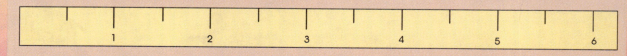

I Can Do It!

102

Skills Assessment

©2001 by Evan-Moor Corp. • Math Practice at Home • EMC 4517

How Many Flowers?

Write multiplication problems to show how many flowers.
Then solve each problem.

_____ x _____ = _____

_____ x _____ = _____

_____ x _____ = _____

_____ x _____ = _____

Multiplication Facts

In the Garden

Harvest of Addition and Subtraction

59	72	43	73	46	60
+ 24	+ 16	+ 46	+ 55	+ 44	+ 39

36	53	99	41	62	50
− 14	− 14	− 11	− 29	− 33	− 25

222	432	612	668	790	576
− 200	+ 135	+ 243	− 240	− 190	− 251

5	2	5	1	6	2
4	2	5	9	4	3
4	2	5	8	7	4
6	2	5	2	3	5
2	2	5	2	8	2
+ 8	+ 2	+ 5	+ 8	+ 2	+ 1

Two- and Three-Digit Addition & Subtraction w/wo Regrouping; Column Add.

Farmer Smith's Rain Gauges

It is important for Farmer Smith to know how much rain his crops are getting. He measures every rainfall.

Here are his rain records for 7 days. The gauges show rainfall in inches.

Make a graph to show the information.

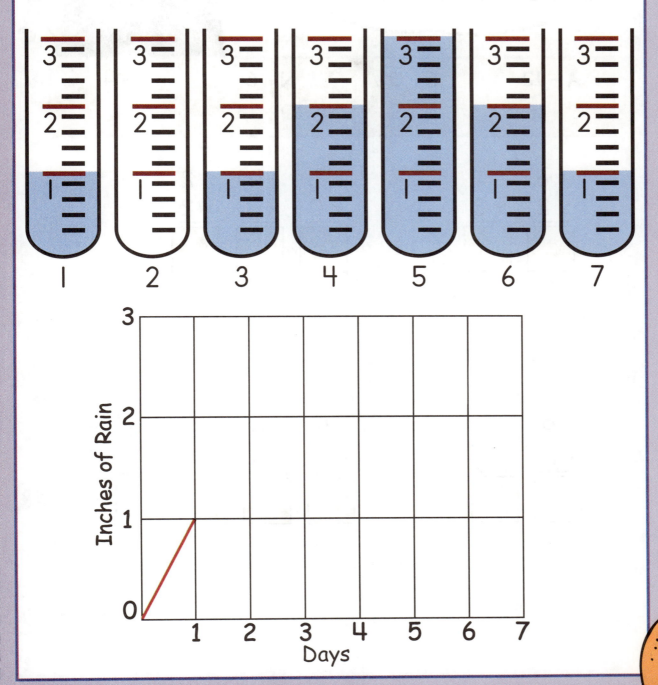

A Garden Riddle

You throw away the outside and cook the inside. Then you eat the outside and throw away the inside. What is it?

A – 12	E – 0	N – 6	R – 4
C – 16	F – 9	O – 18	

$$\begin{array}{cc} 6 & 2 \\ \times 2 & \times 3 \end{array}$$

$$\begin{array}{ccc} 5 & 4 & 2 \\ \times 0 & \times 3 & \times 2 \end{array}$$

$$\begin{array}{cc} 9 & 3 \\ \times 2 & \times 3 \end{array}$$

$$\begin{array}{cccc} 4 & 6 & 1 & 1 \\ \times 4 & \times 3 & \times 4 & \times 6 \end{array}$$

Planting a Flower Garden

Write each problem. Then solve it.

Elisa is planting bulbs. She bought 5 bags of tulip bulbs. There are 5 bulbs in each bag. How many bulbs will she plant?

_____ bulbs

Jamal wants to plant 25 daffodils. He bought 6 bags, each with 4 bulbs. Does he have the number he wants to plant?

_____

Ian wants to plant iris. Iris are sold in bags of 3. He bought 4 bags. How many iris will Ian plant?

_____ iris

There are ten bags of crocus on the shelf. Each bag holds 10 bulbs. How many crocus bulbs are there?

_____ crocus bulbs

Jennifer is planting paper whites. She dug 10 holes. She has 6 bags with 2 bulbs in each bag. How many more holes must she dig?

_____ holes

©2001 by Evan-Moor Corp. • Math Practice at Home • EMC 4517

Solving Word Problems

In the Garden

Picking for Pennies

Penny's mom has a garden. Penny earns money picking fruits and vegetables. Here is yesterday's harvest.

Complete the table to show what Penny earned yesterday.

Crop	Amount Picked	Amount Paid for Each	Amount Earned
Strawberries		2¢	
Tomatoes		3¢	
Pumpkins		5¢	
Corn		4¢	
Beans		1¢	

How much did Penny earn in all? _____

Solving Word Problems; Completing a Chart

In the Garden

Sort the Seeds

Paste each problem in the seed packet where it belongs.

©2001 by Evan-Moor Corp. • Math Practice at Home • EMC 4517

8 × 2

6 × 2

4 × 4

4 × 3

4 × 5

4 × 2

8 × 1

10 × 2

Multiplication Facts

109

Harvest Time

Solve the problems to see how many of each vegetable Farmer Fred harvested.

6
x 2

3
x 3

4
x 2

1 x 4 = ____

3 x 4 = ____

5 x 5 = ____

2 x 0 = ____

5 x 3 = ____

2 x 3 = ____

How many green vegetables? _____

How many red vegetables? _____

How many yellow vegetables? _____

How many orange vegetables? _____

Multiplication Facts; Addition

Roberto keeps track of the time each of his garden chores takes.

Here is his record for last Saturday. How much time did he spend on each task?

Weeding

Start	Stop	How much time?
		_____ : _____

Watering

Start	Stop	How much time?
		_____ : _____

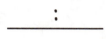

Planting and Pruning

Start	Stop	How much time?
		_____ : _____

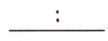

Picking Ripe Fruits & Vegetables

Start	Stop	How much time?
		_____ : _____

★Super Bonus: How much time did Roberto spend in the garden last Saturday? _____

In the Garden

How Does Your Garden Grow?

Write each problem. Then solve it.

Don wants to plant 24 carrot plants. He has planted 15. How many more carrots does he need to plant?

_____ carrots

Jan planted 150 lettuce plants on Saturday. She has 126 left to plant on Sunday. How many plants will she have planted in all?

_____ plants

Ron picked 21 cucumbers one day and 29 cucumbers a week later. How many cucumbers has he picked?

_____ cucumbers

Fred has 4 baskets of strawberries. There are 10 berries in each basket. How many berries are there in all?

_____ berries

Shelley made a fruit basket for a friend. The basket held four oranges, six apples, five bananas, and five pears. How much fruit was in the basket?

_____ pieces of fruit

Gardening Patterns

Every gardener has a way they like to plant the rows in their gardens. Look at each gardener's pattern and label it.

_____

_____

_____

How would you plant your garden?
Draw and label your pattern.

Labeling and Creating Patterns

In the Garden

Apples to Apples

__2__ sets of __4__ apples

__2__ x __4__ = __8__

__4__ sets of __2__ apples

__4__ x __2__ = __8__

____ set of ____ apples

____ x ____ = ____

____ sets of ____ apple

____ x ____ = ____

____ sets of ____ apples

____ x ____ = ____

____ sets of ____ apples

____ x ____ = ____

Does the number order in multiplication change the answer? _____

Commutative Property of Multiplication   ©2001 by Evan-Moor Corp. • Math Practice at Home • EMC 4517

You have reached the last unit in this book. It will review most of the math skills you did in Units 1–9. At the end of Unit 10 is a 2-page I Can Do It! that will help you see how well you know the math skills in this book. Good luck!

9 + 9	5 + 8	13 − 4	8 + 4	14 − 5	18 − 9
16 − 8	8 + 7	14 − 6	7 + 6	9 + 6	15 − 9
13 − 6	12 − 3	9 + 4	7 + 9	9 + 5	15 − 6
16 − 7	13 − 5	17 − 8	8 − 8	4 + 9	12 − 8
9 5 + 1	8 4 + 2	7 7 + 4	9 8 + 0	4 9 + 4	6 3 + 4

The Beautiful Sea

Beach Geometry

What is the perimeter of each figure?

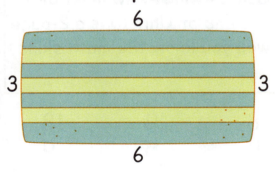

6
3   3
6

3   3
3   3
3   3
3   3
3   3

_____

5   5
1   1
2 3   3 2
4   4
7

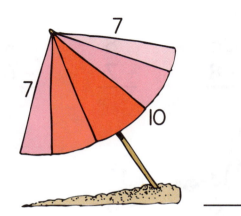

7
7
10

_____

_____

Are the two parts of each figure symmetrical?

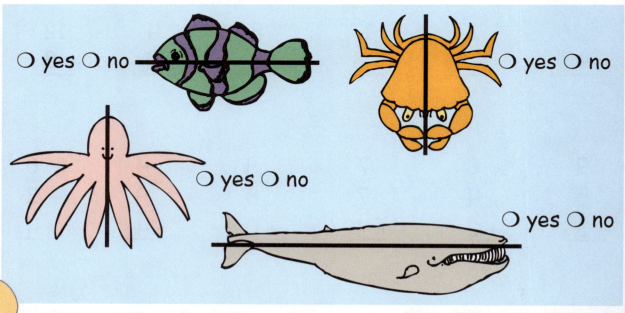

○ yes ○ no

○ yes ○ no

○ yes ○ no

○ yes ○ no

Perimeter; Symmetry   ©2001 by Evan-Moor Corp. • Math Practice at Home • EMC 4517

The Beautiful Sea

Write each problem. Then solve it.

Bo and Jo were collecting shells at the beach. Bo took home 23 shells. Jo took home 29 shells. How many shells did they collect together?

_____ shells

We counted mussels on 8 rocks in the tide pool. There were 3 mussels on each rock. How many mussels were there?

_____ mussels

We saw 34 crabs scurrying along the beach. A big wave took 16 crabs out to sea. How many crabs were left on the beach?

_____ crabs

The octopus ate 4 crabs each day for 5 days. How many crabs did the octopus eat?

_____ crabs

I counted the floats on four strands of seaweed. Here is my count: 5 floats, 7 floats, 4 floats, 3 floats. How many floats in all?

_____ floats

My seashell collection is too big. I gave my friend Rod 27 of my 75 shells. How many shells are left in my collection?

_____ shells

The Beautiful Sea

Measurement Review

A bat ray measures 30 inches across. About how many centimeters would it measure?

○ 30   ○ 25   ○ 15   ○ 75

I measured the height of my sandcastle in both inches and centimeters. Which measurement would show the larger number of units?

○ inches   ○ centimeters

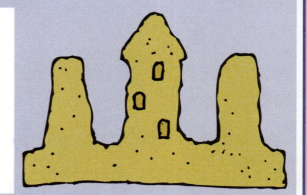

A sea snail crawled 24 inches in 15 minutes. About how far would that be in centimeters?

○ 30   ○ 60   ○ 25   ○ 40

A shell is 5 centimeters long. About how many inches is that? (Look at the rulers below.) About _____ inches.

Inches

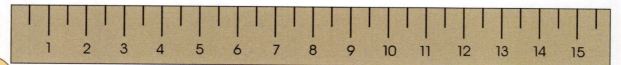

Centimeters

Measuring in Inches and Centimeters   ©2001 by Evan-Moor Corp. • Math Practice at Home • EMC 4517

Two-Digit Addition and Subtraction

$$\begin{array}{r} 20 \\ + 60 \\ \hline \end{array}$$
$$\begin{array}{r} 19 \\ + 22 \\ \hline \end{array}$$
$$\begin{array}{r} 55 \\ + 35 \\ \hline \end{array}$$
$$\begin{array}{r} 10 \\ + 81 \\ \hline \end{array}$$
$$\begin{array}{r} 29 \\ + 39 \\ \hline \end{array}$$

$$\begin{array}{r} 38 \\ - 21 \\ \hline \end{array}$$
$$\begin{array}{r} 44 \\ - 32 \\ \hline \end{array}$$
$$\begin{array}{r} 32 \\ - 13 \\ \hline \end{array}$$
$$\begin{array}{r} 43 \\ - 27 \\ \hline \end{array}$$
$$\begin{array}{r} 97 \\ - 19 \\ \hline \end{array}$$
$$\begin{array}{r} 45 \\ - 26 \\ \hline \end{array}$$

$$\begin{array}{r} 72 \\ - 27 \\ \hline \end{array}$$
$$\begin{array}{r} 66 \\ + 26 \\ \hline \end{array}$$
$$\begin{array}{r} 52 \\ + 47 \\ \hline \end{array}$$
$$\begin{array}{r} 66 \\ - 22 \\ \hline \end{array}$$
$$\begin{array}{r} 43 \\ - 29 \\ \hline \end{array}$$
$$\begin{array}{r} 55 \\ - 49 \\ \hline \end{array}$$

$$\begin{array}{r} 77 \\ - 27 \\ \hline \end{array}$$
$$\begin{array}{r} 76 \\ + 18 \\ \hline \end{array}$$
$$\begin{array}{r} 38 \\ + 27 \\ \hline \end{array}$$
$$\begin{array}{r} 30 \\ - 11 \\ \hline \end{array}$$
$$\begin{array}{r} 33 \\ - 25 \\ \hline \end{array}$$
$$\begin{array}{r} 80 \\ - 11 \\ \hline \end{array}$$

$$\begin{array}{r} 68 \\ - 21 \\ \hline \end{array}$$
$$\begin{array}{r} 71 \\ + 19 \\ \hline \end{array}$$
$$\begin{array}{r} 50 \\ - 34 \\ \hline \end{array}$$
$$\begin{array}{r} 37 \\ + 37 \\ \hline \end{array}$$
$$\begin{array}{r} 45 \\ + 24 \\ \hline \end{array}$$
$$\begin{array}{r} 29 \\ - 10 \\ \hline \end{array}$$

The Beautiful Sea

Order and Patterns

This school of fish will help you review numbers and patterns.

Write to tell the order.

second   fifth   first   third   fourth

_____

_____

_____

_____

_____

What is the pattern?

_____

Color these fish to show the pattern ABCBC.

Ordinal Numbers; Patterns

The Beautiful Sea

The Beautiful Sea

I'm a strange-looking shark. In fact, my head looks like a tool used to build things. What is my name?

A – 85	D – 92	E – 76	H – 46
K – 59	M – 27	R – 38	S – 63

94
− 48
☐

49
+ 36
☐

76
− 49
☐

64
− 37
☐

48
+ 28
☐

84
− 46
☐

82
− 36
☐

37
+ 39
☐

47
+ 38
☐

64
+ 28
☐

25
+ 38
☐

63
− 17
☐

26
+ 59
☐

90
− 52
☐

92
− 33
☐

Which one do I look like?

Two-Digit Addition and Subtraction w/wo Regrouping

Money and Time

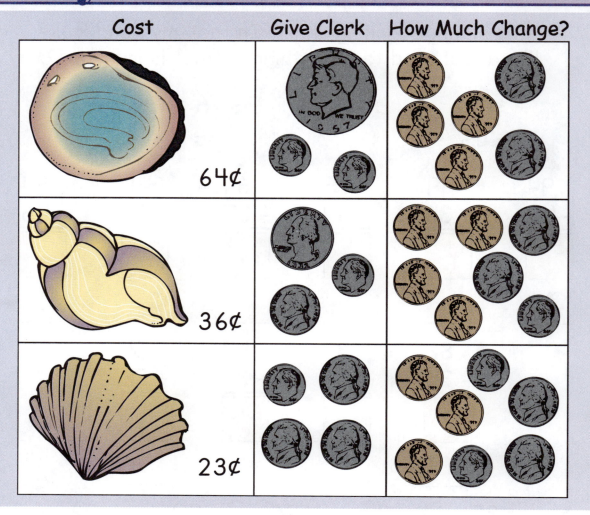

Cost	Give Clerk	How Much Change?

Match.

1:25 •

8:30 •

10:45 •

2:15 •

Value of Coins; Making Change; Telling Time to Five Minutes   ©2001 by Evan-Moor Corp. • Math Practice at Home • EMC 4517

The Beautiful Sea

Three-Digit Addition and Subtraction

```
  689        655        735
- 465      - 324      - 123
```

```
  252        405        721
+ 346      + 550      +  75
```

```
  488      958      777      105      263
- 408    - 427    - 453    + 382    + 336
```

```
  500      687      153      692      200
+ 326    - 445    + 443    - 290    + 199
```

Knowing Numbers

Circle the tens. Box the ones.

52	85
17	92
48	37

Before and After

____, 100, 101

52, ____, 54

88, 89, ____

Connect the dots. Count by 2s.

Place Value; Counting by 2s; Number Order

©2001 by Evan-Moor Corp. • Math Practice at Home • EMC 4517

The Beautiful Sea

$3 \times 4 = \underline{\quad}$ $2 \times 2 = \underline{\quad}$ $3 \times 2 = \underline{\quad}$

$5 \times 2 = \underline{\quad}$ $1 \times 3 = \underline{\quad}$ $4 \times 3 = \underline{\quad}$

$6 \times 3 = \underline{\quad}$ $2 \times 4 = \underline{\quad}$ $5 \times 4 = \underline{\quad}$

$$\begin{array}{cccccc}
8 & 4 & 9 & 7 & 3 & 7 \\
\times 2 & \times 4 & \times 2 & \times 0 & \times 5 & \times 3 \\
\hline
\end{array}$$

$$\begin{array}{cccccc}
6 & 1 & 3 & 4 & 8 & 5 \\
\times 4 & \times 5 & \times 3 & \times 2 & \times 3 & \times 0 \\
\hline
\end{array}$$

$$\begin{array}{cccccc}
5 & 6 & 4 & 3 & 3 & 5 \\
\times 5 & \times 2 & \times 5 & \times 1 & \times 6 & \times 3 \\
\hline
\end{array}$$

Multiplication Facts to 25

Fishy Fractions

Color the fractional amount of each school of fish.

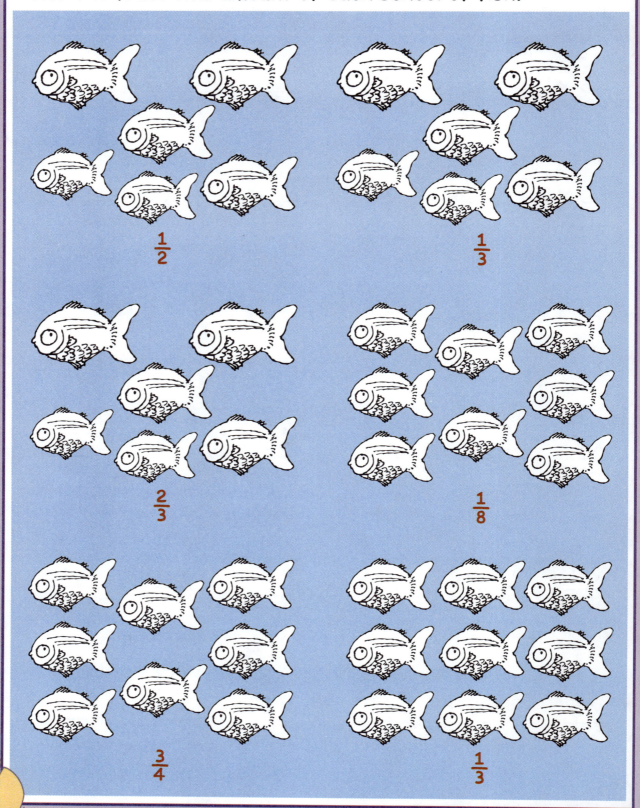

$\frac{1}{2}$

$\frac{1}{3}$

$\frac{2}{3}$

$\frac{1}{8}$

$\frac{3}{4}$

$\frac{1}{3}$

Geometric Shapes; Fractions of a Set

The Beautiful Sea

Match.

seventy-two•   •400

four hundred•   •96

ninety-six•   •72

Before and After

____ 100 ____

____ 69 ____

____ 750 ____

>, <, or = ?

75 ◯ 92

4 + 5 ◯ 14 - 5

157 ◯ 155

Add or subtract.

| 452 | 95 | 361 | 57 | 48 | 82 |
| + 347 | - 49 | + 438 | + 18 | + 38 | - 47 |

Multiply.

5 x 3 = ____   3 x 0 = ____   6 x 2 = ____   1 x 4 = ____

| 7 | 5 | 4 | 2 | 2 | 3 |
| x 2 | x 5 | x 2 | x 1 | x 2 | x 3 |

Continue the pattern. Label it.

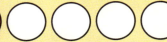   _____

Write the fraction.

_____

Color the fraction. ½

I Can Do It!

Skills Assessment   **127**

I Can Do It!

What time is it?

____:____   ____:____

Match.

square •

cube •

rectangle •

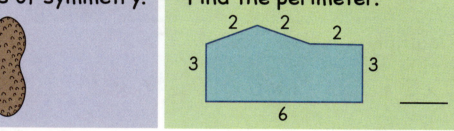

Measure.

_____ ____ inches

_____ ____ centimeters

Draw 2 lines of symmetry.

Find the perimeter.

2   2   2

3   3

6

____

Make a graph.

Team	Games Won
Tigers	8
Bears	4
Lions	6
Bobcats	7

Write the problem. Then solve it.

Brian divided his animal stamps into piles of 5. He had 5 piles. How many animal stamps did Brian have?

____ animal stamps

You are a star!

name:

You have completed this book.

Answer Key

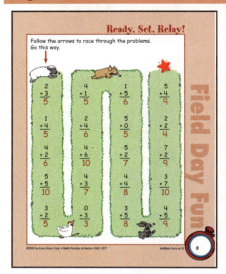

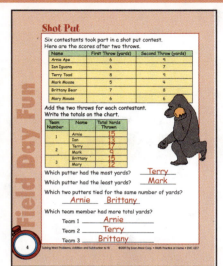

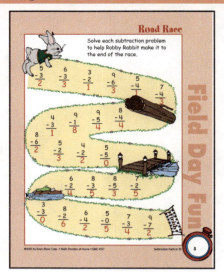

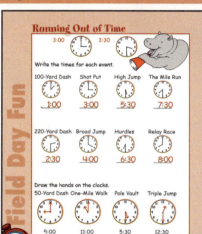

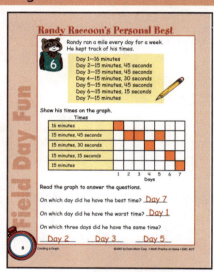

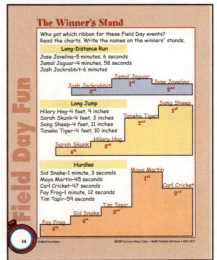

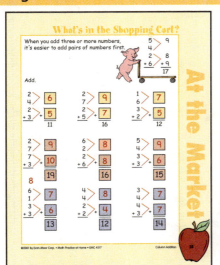

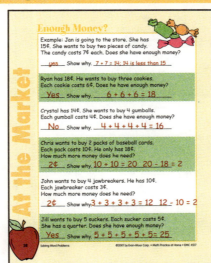

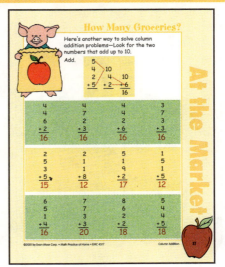

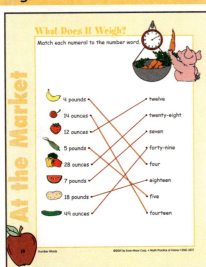

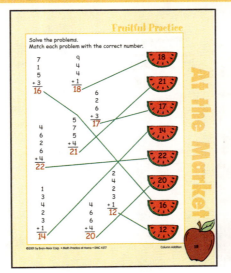

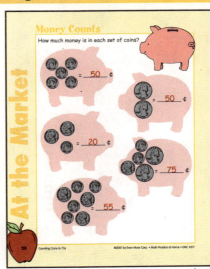

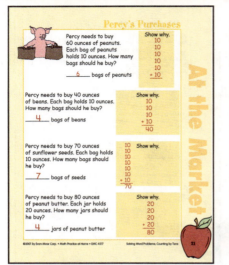

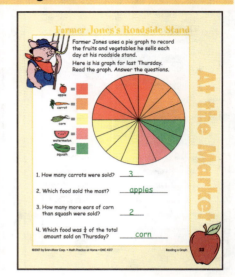

Page 21 **Page 22** **Page 23**

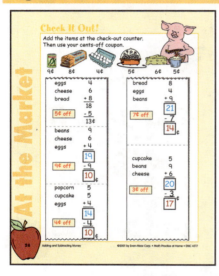

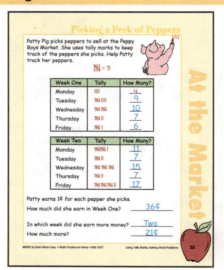

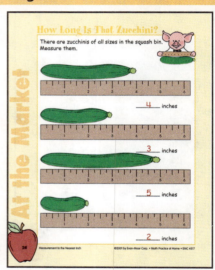

Page 24 **Page 25** **Page 26**

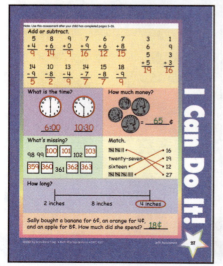

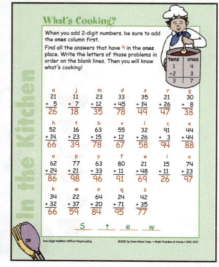

Page 27 **Page 28** **Page 29**

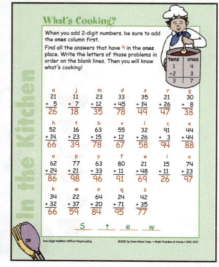

132

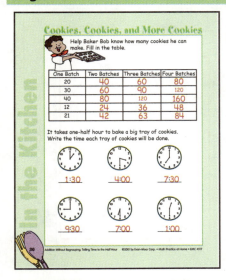

Cookies, Cookies, and More Cookies

Help Baker Bob know how many cookies he can make. Fill in the table.

One Batch	Two Batches	Three Batches	Four Batches
20	40	60	80
30	60	90	120
40	80	120	160
12	24	36	48
21	42	63	84

It takes one-half hour to bake a big tray of cookies. Write the time each tray of cookies will be done.

1:30   4:00   7:30

9:30   7:00   1:00

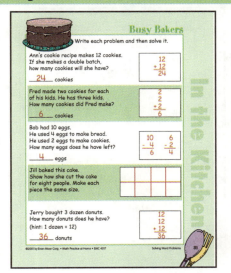

Busy Bakers

Write each problem and then solve it.

Ann's cookie recipe makes 12 cookies. If she makes a double batch, how many cookies will she have?

$$\begin{array}{r} 12 \\ +12 \\ \hline 24 \end{array}$$

24 cookies

Fred made two cookies for each of his kids. He has three kids. How many cookies did Fred make?

$$\begin{array}{r} 2 \\ 2 \\ +2 \\ \hline 6 \end{array}$$

6 cookies

Bob had 10 eggs. He used 4 eggs to make bread. He used 2 eggs to make cookies. How many eggs does he have left?

$$\begin{array}{r} 10 \\ -4 \\ \hline 6 \end{array} \quad \begin{array}{r} 6 \\ -2 \\ \hline 4 \end{array}$$

4 eggs

Jill baked this cake. Show how she cut the cake for eight people. Make each piece the same size.

Jerry bought 3 dozen donuts. How many donuts does he have? (hint: 1 dozen = 12)

$$\begin{array}{r} 12 \\ 12 \\ +12 \\ \hline 36 \end{array}$$

36 donuts

Measure It!

Measure the milk. Color to show the right amount.

1½ cups   1¼ cups

¼ cup   2¼ cups

Measure the butter. Color to show the right amount.

1½ sticks

¾ stick

2½ sticks

1½ sticks

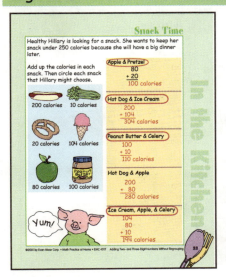

Snack Time

Healthy Hillary is looking for a snack. She wants to keep her snack under 250 calories because she will have a big dinner later.

Add up the calories in each snack. Then circle each snack that Hillary might choose.

200 calories   10 calories

20 calories   104 calories

80 calories   100 calories

Yum!

Apple & Pretzel
$$\begin{array}{r} 80 \\ +20 \\ \hline 100 \end{array}$$ calories

Hot Dog & Ice Cream
$$\begin{array}{r} 200 \\ +104 \\ \hline 304 \end{array}$$ calories

Peanut Butter & Celery
$$\begin{array}{r} 100 \\ +10 \\ \hline 110 \end{array}$$ calories

Hot Dog & Apple
$$\begin{array}{r} 200 \\ +80 \\ \hline 280 \end{array}$$ calories

Ice Cream, Apple, & Celery
$$\begin{array}{r} 104 \\ 80 \\ +10 \\ \hline 194 \end{array}$$ calories

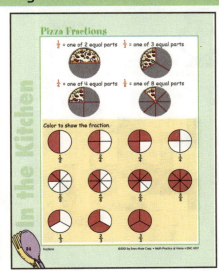

Pizza Fractions

½ = one of 2 equal parts   ⅓ = one of 3 equal parts

¼ = one of 4 equal parts   ⅛ = one of 8 equal parts

Color to show the fraction.

½   ¾   ¾   ¼

⅝   ⅘   ⅚   ⅞

⅓   ⅔   ⅓

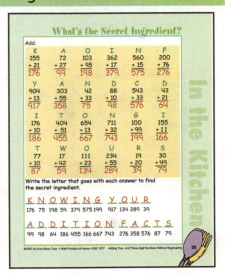

What's the Secret Ingredient?

Add.

K	A	O	I	N	F
155	72	103	362	560	200
+21	+27	+95	+17	+15	+76
176	99	198	379	575	276

Y	A	N	D	C	D
904	303	42	88	543	43
+13	+55	+33	+10	+33	+21
917	358	75	98	576	64

I	T	O	N	G	I
176	404	654	711	100	155
+10	+51	+13	+32	+99	+11
186	455	667	743	199	166

T	W	O	U	R	S
77	17	111	234	19	30
+10	+42	+23	+55	+20	+49
87	59	134	289	39	79

Write the letter that goes with each answer to find the secret ingredient.

K N O W I N G   Y O U R
176 75 134 59 379 575 199   917 134 289 39

A D D I T I O N   F A C T S
99 98 64 186 455 166 667 743   276 358 576 87 79

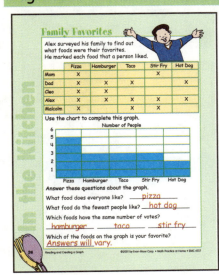

Family Favorites

Alex surveyed his family to find out what foods were their favorites. He marked each food that a person liked.

	Pizza	Hamburger	Taco	Stir Fry	Hot Dog
Mom	X			X	
Dad	X	X	X		X
Cleo	X	X			
Alex	X	X	X	X	
Malcolm	X		X	X	

Use the chart to complete this graph.

Number of People

Answer these questions about the graph.

What food does everyone like? **pizza**

What food do the fewest people like? **hot dog**

Which foods have the same number of votes?

hamburger   taco   stir fry

Which of the foods on the graph is your favorite?

Answers will vary.

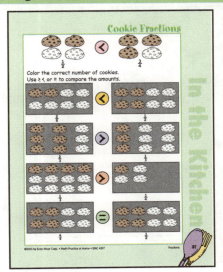

Cookie Fractions

½   ¾

Color the correct number of cookies. Use >, <, or = to compare the amounts.

⅓ < ⅔

⅝ > ⅜

¾ > ¼

2/4 = ½

What Did You Eat?

Your meal cost $8.00. What did you eat?

Menu
Hot Dog $4.00   Hamburger $5.00
Sandwich $7.00   Chips $1.00

Show your work.
$$\begin{array}{r} \$7.00 \\ +\ 1.00 \\ \hline \$8.00 \end{array}$$

sandwich and chips

Your meal cost $10.00. What did you eat?

Menu
Pizza $7.00   Drink $2.00
Salad $3.00   Ice Cream $4.00

Show your work.
$$\begin{array}{r} \$7.00 \\ +\ 3.00 \\ \hline \$10.00 \end{array}$$

pizza and salad

Your meal cost $12.00. What did you eat?

Menu
Taco $2.00   Burrito $3.00
Corn Chips $1.00   Nachos $7.00

Show your work.
$$\begin{array}{r} \$2.00 \\ 3.00 \\ +\ 7.00 \\ \hline \$12.00 \end{array}$$

taco, burrito, and nachos

Page 39 — Cover the Table

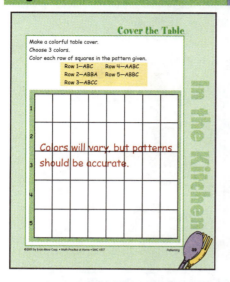

In the Kitchen

Make a colorful table cover.
Choose 3 colors.
Color each row of squares in the pattern given.

Row 1—ABC   Row 4—AABC
Row 2—ABBA   Row 5—ABBC
Row 3—ABCC

Colors will vary, but patterns should be accurate.

Page 40 — Just Ducky!

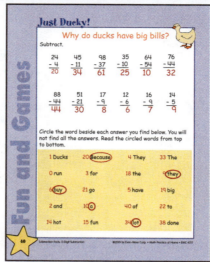

Fun and Games

Why do ducks have big bills?

Subtract.

24 − 4 = 20	45 − 11 = 34	98 − 37 = 61	35 − 10 = 25	64 − 54 = 10	76 − 44 = 32
88 − 44 = 44	51 − 21 = 30	17 − 9 = 8	12 − 6 = 6	16 − 9 = 7	14 − 5 = 9

Circle the word beside each answer you find below. You will not find all the answers. Read the circled words from top to bottom.

1 Ducks	20 Because	4 They	33 The
0 run	3 for	18 the	9 they
6 buy	21 go	5 have	19 big
2 and	10 a	40 of	22 to
14 hot	15 fun	34 lot	38 done

Page 41 — Just the Same

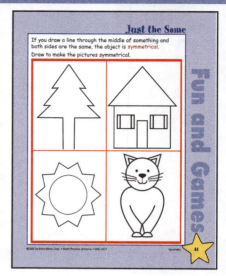

Fun and Games

If you draw a line through the middle of something and both sides are the same, the object is symmetrical.
Draw to make the pictures symmetrical.

Page 42 — Can You Believe Your Eyes?

Fun and Games

Color answers that end in:

0 green   2 purple   4 red
1 blue   3 violet   5 orange

783 − 83 = 700	881 − 70 = 811	777 − 25 = 752	896 − 753 = 143	856 − 432 = 424	196 − 81 = 115

Page 43 — Which Ride?

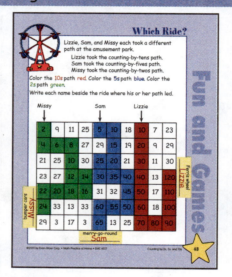

Fun and Games

Lizzie, Sam, and Missy each took a different path at the amusement park.
Lizzie took the counting-by-tens path.
Sam took the counting-by-fives path.
Missy took the counting-by-twos path.
Color the 10s path red. Color the 5s path blue. Color the 2s path green.
Write each name beside the ride where his or her path led.

Missy   Sam   Lizzie

Ferris wheel — Lizzie
bumper cars — Missy
merry-go-round — Sam

Page 44 — Basketball Pointers

Fun and Games

Write each problem. Then solve it.

The Bulldogs basketball team ended the game with 76 points. The Tigers had 66 points. By how many points did the Bulldogs win?

10 points

The Lions had 46 points at the end of the game. They made 24 points in the first half. How many points did they make in the second half?

22 points

The Bulldogs played nine players in the first half and eight different players in the second half. How many Bulldogs played in the game?

17 players

The Tigers' score was 24. That score was 64 points less than the Bulldogs' score. What was the Bulldogs' score?

88 points

The Bulldogs bought three new basketballs for the game. Each ball cost $20.00. How much did the team spend?

$60.00

The clock showed 55 seconds left in the game. The next play took 32 seconds. How many seconds were left in the game?

23 seconds

Page 45 — Round Up the Bucks

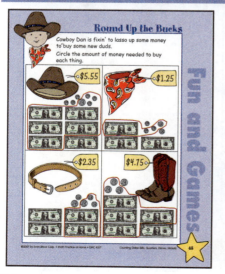

Fun and Games

Cowboy Dan is fixin' to lasso up some money to buy some new duds.
Circle the amount of money needed to buy each thing.

$5.55 $1.25 $2.35 $4.75

Page 46 — A Goofy Riddle

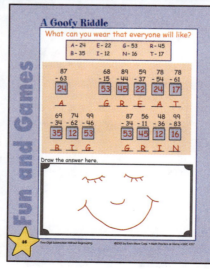

Fun and Games

What can you wear that everyone will like?

A - 24   E - 22   G - 53   R - 45
B - 35   I - 12   N - 16   T - 17

87 − 63 = 24	68 − 15 = 53	89 − 44 = 45	59 − 37 = 22	78 − 54 = 24	78 − 61 = 17
A	G	R	E	A	T

69 − 34 = 35	74 − 62 = 12	99 − 46 = 53	87 − 34 = 53	56 − 11 = 45	48 − 36 = 12	99 − 83 = 16
B	I	G	G	R	I	N

Draw the answer here.

Page 47 — Cross the River

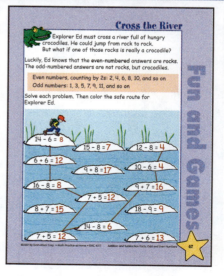

Fun and Games

Explorer Ed must cross a river full of hungry crocodiles. He could jump from rock to rock. But what if one of those rocks is really a crocodile?

Luckily, Ed knows that the even-numbered answers are rocks. The odd-numbered answers are not rocks, but crocodiles.

Even numbers, counting by 2s: 2, 4, 6, 8, 10, and so on
Odd numbers: 1, 3, 5, 7, 9, 11, and so on

Solve each problem. Then color the safe route for Explorer Ed.

14 − 6 = 8   15 − 8 = 7   12 − 8 = 4
6 + 6 = 12   9 + 8 = 17   10 − 6 = 4
16 − 8 = 8   9 + 7 = 16
8 + 7 = 15   7 + 5 = 12   18 − 9 = 9
7 + 5 = 12   14 − 8 = 6   7 + 6 = 13

134

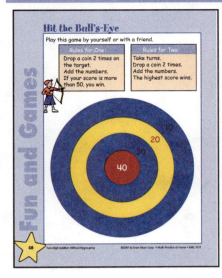

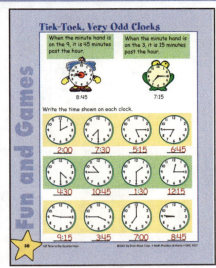

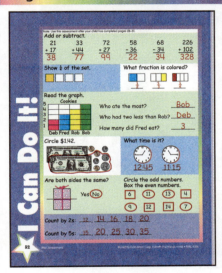

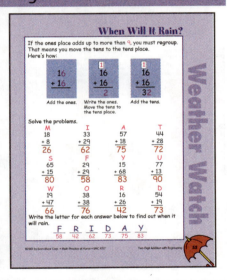

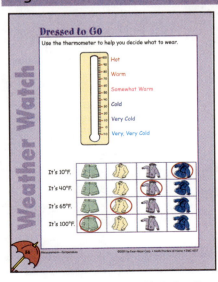

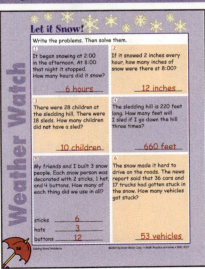

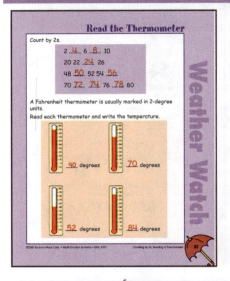

Read the Thermometer

Count by 2s.

2 _4_ 6 _8_ 10
20 22 _24_ 26
48 _50_ 52 54 _56_
70 _72_ _74_ 76 _78_ 80

A Fahrenheit thermometer is usually marked in 2-degree units.
Read each thermometer and write the temperature.

_90_ degrees   _70_ degrees

_52_ degrees   _84_ degrees

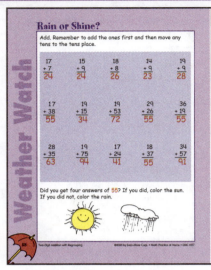

Rain or Shine?

Add. Remember to add the ones first and then move any tens to the tens place.

17	15	18	14	19
+ 7	+ 9	+ 8	+ 9	+ 9
24	24	26	23	28

17	19	19	29	36
+ 38	+ 15	+ 53	+ 26	+ 19
55	34	72	55	55

28	19	17	18	34
+ 35	+ 75	+ 24	+ 37	+ 57
63	94	41	55	91

Did you get four answers of 55? If you did, color the sun.
If you did not, color the rain.

Foul-Weather Gear

Color to show the fractions.

1/2
1/3
1/4
2/3
1/4

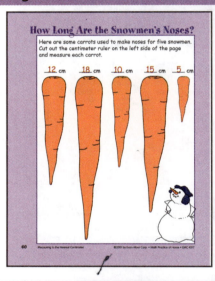

How Long Are the Snowmen's Noses?

Here are some carrots used to make noses for five snowmen.
Cut out the centimeter ruler on the left side of the page
and measure each carrot.

_12_ cm   _18_ cm   _10_ cm   _15_ cm   _5_ cm

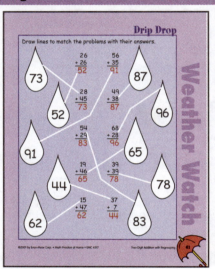

Drip Drop

Draw lines to match the problems with their answers.

26	56
+ 26	+ 35
52	91

73   87

28	49
+ 45	+ 38
73	87

52   96

54	68
+ 29	+ 28
83	96

91   65

19	39
+ 46	+ 39
65	78

44   78

15	37
+ 47	+ 7
62	44

62   83

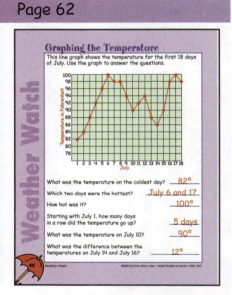

Graphing the Temperature

This line graph shows the temperature for the first 18 days
of July. Use the graph to answer the questions.

What was the temperature on the coldest day? _82°_
Which two days were the hottest? _July 6 and 17_
How hot was it? _100°_
Starting with July 1, how many days
in a row did the temperature go up? _5 days_
What was the temperature on July 10? _90°_
What was the difference between the
temperatures on July 14 and July 16? _12°_

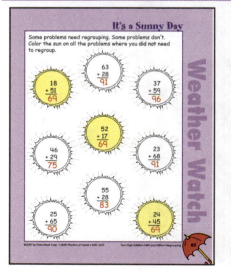

It's a Sunny Day

Some problems need regrouping. Some problems don't.
Color the sun on all the problems where you did not
need to regroup.

18	63	37
+ 51	+ 28	+ 59
69	91	96

46	52	23
+ 29	+ 17	+ 68
75	69	91

25	55	24
+ 65	+ 28	+ 45
90	83	69

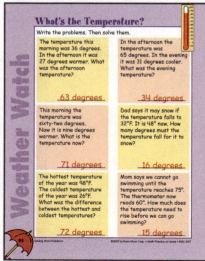

What's the Temperature?

Write the problems. Then solve them.

The temperature this morning was 36 degrees. In the afternoon it was 27 degrees warmer. What was the afternoon temperature?

63 degrees

In the afternoon the temperature was 65 degrees. In the evening it was 31° cooler. What was the evening temperature?

34 degrees

This morning the temperature was sixty-two degrees. Now it is nine degrees warmer. What is the temperature now?

71 degrees

Dad says it may snow if the temperature falls to 32°F. It is 48° now. How many degrees must the temperature fall for it to snow?

16 degrees

The hottest temperature of the year was 98°F. The coldest temperature of the year was 26°F. What was the difference between the hottest and coldest temperatures?

72 degrees

Mom says we cannot go swimming until the temperature reaches 75°. The thermometer now reads 60°. How much does the temperature need to rise before we can go swimming?

15 degrees

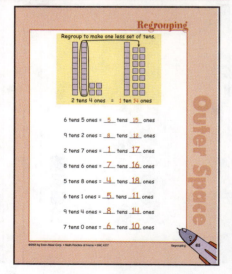

Regrouping

Regroup to make one less set of tens.

2 tens 4 ones = 1 ten 14 ones

6 tens 5 ones = _5_ tens _15_ ones
9 tens 2 ones = _8_ tens _12_ ones
2 tens 7 ones = _1_ ten _17_ ones
8 tens 6 ones = _7_ tens _16_ ones
5 tens 8 ones = _4_ tens _18_ ones
6 tens 1 ones = _5_ tens _11_ ones
9 tens 4 ones = _8_ tens _14_ ones
7 tens 0 ones = _6_ tens _10_ ones

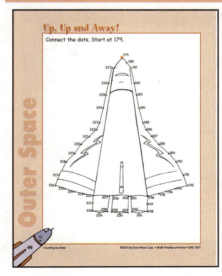

Up, Up and Away!

Connect the dots. Start at 179.

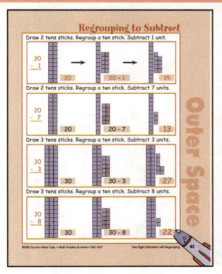

Regrouping to Subtract

Draw 2 tens sticks. Regroup a ten stick. Subtract 1 unit.

$$\begin{array}{r} 20 \\ -\ 1 \\ \hline \end{array}$$ 20   20 - 1   **19**

Draw 2 tens sticks. Regroup a ten stick. Subtract 7 units.

$$\begin{array}{r} 20 \\ -\ 7 \\ \hline \end{array}$$ 20   20 - 7   **13**

Draw 3 tens sticks. Regroup a ten stick. Subtract 3 units.

$$\begin{array}{r} 30 \\ -\ 3 \\ \hline \end{array}$$ 30   30 - 3   **27**

Draw 3 tens sticks. Regroup a ten stick. Subtract 8 units.

$$\begin{array}{r} 30 \\ -\ 8 \\ \hline \end{array}$$ 30   30 - 8   **22**

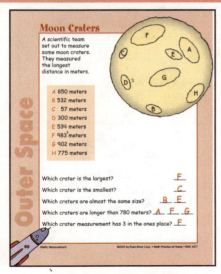

Moon Craters

A scientific team set out to measure some moon craters. They measured the longest distance in meters.

A 850 meters
B 532 meters
C 57 meters
D 300 meters
E 534 meters
F 983 meters
G 902 meters
H 775 meters

Which crater is the largest? **F**
Which crater is the smallest? **C**
Which craters are almost the same size? **B   E**
Which craters are longer than 780 meters? **A   F   G**
Which crater measurement has 3 in the ones place? **F**

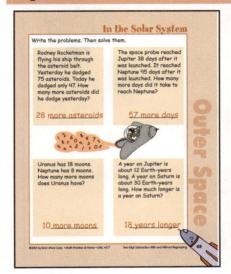

In the Solar System

Write the problems. Then solve them.

Rodney Rocketman is flying his ship through the asteroid belt. Yesterday he dodged 75 asteroids. Today he dodged only 47. How many more asteroids did he dodge yesterday?

28 more asteroids

The space probe reached Jupiter 38 days after it was launched. It reached Neptune 95 days after it was launched. How many more days did it take to reach Neptune?

57 more days

Uranus has 18 moons. Neptune has 8 moons. How many more moons does Uranus have?

10 more moons

A year on Jupiter is about 12 Earth-years long. A year on Saturn is about 30 Earth-years long. How much longer is a year on Saturn?

18 years longer

Subtraction with Regrouping

This is what I think when I need to regroup to subtract:
I can't take 6 away from 4, so I must regroup the tens.
Now I have 2 tens and 14 ones.
14 - 6 = 8
2 tens - 0 tens = 2 tens

$$\begin{array}{r} {}^{2}3\,{}^{1}4 \\ -\ 6 \\ \hline 2\ 8 \end{array}$$

$$\begin{array}{r} {}^{2}30 \\ -\ 3 \\ \hline 27 \end{array} \quad \begin{array}{r} {}^{4}51 \\ -\ 8 \\ \hline 43 \end{array} \quad \begin{array}{r} {}^{3}43 \\ -\ 5 \\ \hline 38 \end{array} \quad \begin{array}{r} {}^{4}50 \\ -\ 7 \\ \hline 43 \end{array} \quad \begin{array}{r} {}^{2}28 \\ -\ 9 \\ \hline 19 \end{array}$$

$$\begin{array}{r} {}^{6}74 \\ -\ 5 \\ \hline 69 \end{array} \quad \begin{array}{r} {}^{3}30 \\ -\ 1 \\ \hline 29 \end{array} \quad \begin{array}{r} {}^{3}34 \\ -\ 9 \\ \hline 25 \end{array} \quad \begin{array}{r} {}^{4}42 \\ -\ 3 \\ \hline 39 \end{array} \quad \begin{array}{r} {}^{2}23 \\ -\ 6 \\ \hline 17 \end{array}$$

$$\begin{array}{r} {}^{2}21 \\ -\ 5 \\ \hline 16 \end{array} \quad \begin{array}{r} {}^{5}64 \\ -\ 9 \\ \hline 55 \end{array} \quad \begin{array}{r} {}^{4}55 \\ -\ 8 \\ \hline 47 \end{array} \quad \begin{array}{r} {}^{3}31 \\ -\ 5 \\ \hline 26 \end{array} \quad \begin{array}{r} {}^{7}77 \\ -\ 9 \\ \hline 68 \end{array}$$

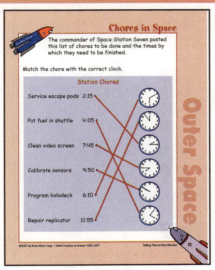

Chores in Space

The commander of Space Station Seven posted this list of chores to be done and the times by which they need to be finished.

Match the chore with the correct clock.

Station Chores

Service escape pods 2:15
Put fuel in shuttle 4:05
Clean video screen 7:45
Calibrate sensors 9:50
Program holodeck 6:10
Repair replicator 11:55

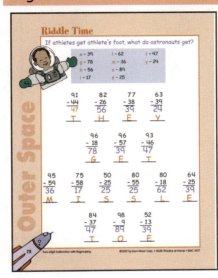

Riddle Time

If athletes get athlete's foot, what do astronauts get?

e - 39   i - 62   t - 47
g - 78   m - 36   y - 24
h - 56   o - 89
l - 17   s - 25

$$\begin{array}{r} 91 \\ -44 \\ \hline 47 \\ T \end{array} \quad \begin{array}{r} 82 \\ -26 \\ \hline 56 \\ H \end{array} \quad \begin{array}{r} 77 \\ -38 \\ \hline 39 \\ E \end{array} \quad \begin{array}{r} 63 \\ -39 \\ \hline 24 \\ Y \end{array}$$

$$\begin{array}{r} 96 \\ -18 \\ \hline 78 \\ G \end{array} \quad \begin{array}{r} 96 \\ -57 \\ \hline 39 \\ E \end{array} \quad \begin{array}{r} 93 \\ -46 \\ \hline 47 \\ T \end{array}$$

$$\begin{array}{r} 95 \\ -59 \\ \hline 36 \\ M \end{array} \quad \begin{array}{r} 75 \\ -58 \\ \hline 17 \\ I \end{array} \quad \begin{array}{r} 50 \\ -25 \\ \hline 25 \\ S \end{array} \quad \begin{array}{r} 80 \\ -55 \\ \hline 25 \\ S \end{array} \quad \begin{array}{r} 80 \\ -18 \\ \hline 62 \\ I \end{array} \quad \begin{array}{r} 64 \\ -25 \\ \hline 39 \\ E \end{array}$$

$$\begin{array}{r} 84 \\ -37 \\ \hline 47 \\ T \end{array} \quad \begin{array}{r} 98 \\ -\ 9 \\ \hline 89 \\ O \end{array} \quad \begin{array}{r} 52 \\ -13 \\ \hline 39 \\ E \end{array}$$

How Many Moons?

Color the graph to show how many moons each planet has.

Mercury - no moons   Mars - 2 moons   Uranus - 18 moons
Venus - no moons   Jupiter - 16 moons   Neptune - 8 moons
Earth - 1 moon   Saturn - 18 moons   Pluto - 1 moon

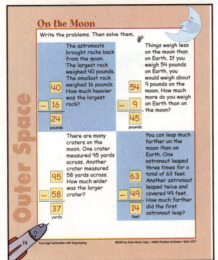

On the Moon

Write the problems. Then solve them.

The astronauts brought rocks back from the moon. The largest rock weighed 40 pounds. The smallest rock weighed 16 pounds. How much heavier was the largest rock?

$$\begin{array}{r} 40 \\ -\ 16 \\ \hline 24 \end{array}$$ pounds

Things weigh less on the moon than on Earth. If you weigh 54 pounds on Earth, you would weigh about 9 pounds on the moon. How much more do you weigh on Earth than on the moon?

$$\begin{array}{r} 54 \\ -\ 9 \\ \hline 45 \end{array}$$ pounds

There are many craters on the moon. One crater measured 95 yards across. Another crater measured 58 yards across. How much wider was the larger crater?

$$\begin{array}{r} 95 \\ -\ 58 \\ \hline 37 \end{array}$$ yards

You can leap much farther on the moon than on Earth. One astronaut leaped three times for a total of 63 feet. Another astronaut leaped twice and covered 49 feet. How much farther did the first astronaut leap?

$$\begin{array}{r} 63 \\ -\ 49 \\ \hline 14 \end{array}$$ feet

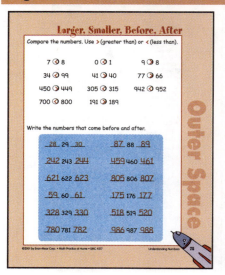

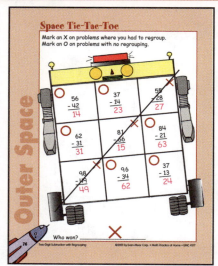

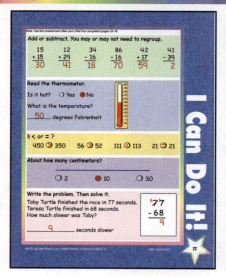

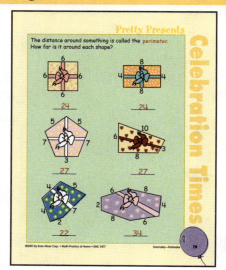

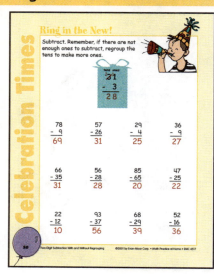

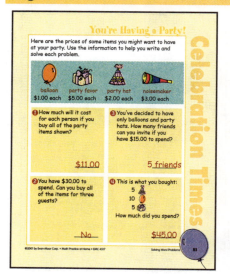

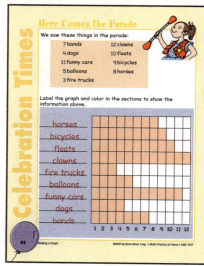

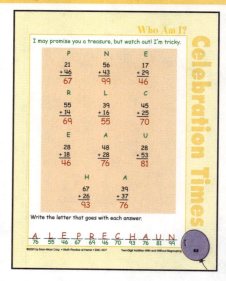

138

Page 84

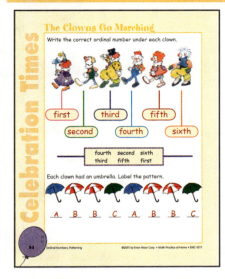

The Clowns Go Marching

Write the correct ordinal number under each clown.

first — second — third — fourth — fifth — sixth

| fourth | second | sixth |
| third | fifth | first |

Each clown had an umbrella. Label the pattern.

A B B C A B B C

Page 85

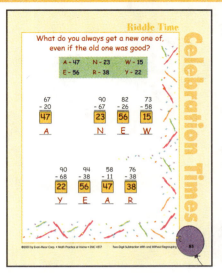

Riddle Time

What do you always get a new one of, even if the old one was good?

| A - 47 | N - 23 | W - 15 |
| E - 56 | R - 38 | Y - 22 |

67 − 20 = **47** A
90 − 67 = **23** N
82 − 26 = **56** E
73 − 58 = **15** W

90 − 68 = **22** Y
94 − 38 = **56** E
58 − 11 = **47** A
76 − 38 = **38** R

Page 86

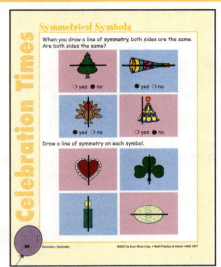

Symmetrical Symbols

When you draw a line of symmetry, both sides are the same. Are both sides the same?

○ yes ● no   ● yes ○ no
● yes ○ no   ○ yes ● no

Draw a line of symmetry on each symbol.

Page 87

A Message for You

Be careful. Some problems require regrouping; some do not. When you are finished, color the squares with problems where you did not regroup.

23 + 46 = 69	75 + 19 = 94	71 + 28 = 99	37 + 28 = 65	65 − 34 = 31
48 − 26 = 22	89 − 25 = 64	99 − 63 = 36	43 − 27 = 16	33 + 66 = 99
57 − 14 = 43	94 − 66 = 28	54 + 35 = 89	66 − 47 = 19	78 − 30 = 48

What is the secret message? _____ Hi

Page 88

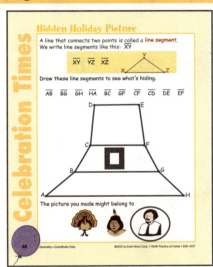

Hidden Holiday Picture

A line that connects two points is called a **line segment**. We write line segments like this: XY

XY YZ XZ

Draw these line segments to see what's hiding.

AB BG GH HA BC GF CF CD DE EF

The picture you made might belong to

Page 89

A Pot of Gold!

Congratulations! You tricked the leprechaun and now you have a pot of gold. How will you spend it?

$74 $18 $57 $85 $46

Write each problem. Then solve it.

The pot of gold has $90.00 in it. How much will you have left if you buy a baseball glove?
$33.00

The pot of gold has $75.00 in it. Can you buy a calculator and a doll?
Yes

How much will be left if the pot of gold has $98 in it and you buy a scooter?
$13.00

You can buy any two of the items pictured. What would you buy? How much would it cost?
Answers will vary.

Page 90

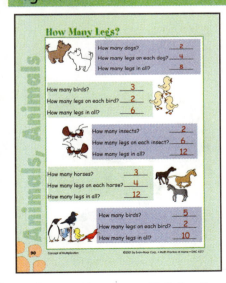

How Many Legs?

How many dogs? 2
How many legs on each dog? 4
How many legs in all? 8

How many birds? 3
How many legs on each bird? 2
How many legs in all? 6

How many insects? 2
How many legs on each insect? 6
How many legs in all? 12

How many horses? 3
How many legs on each horse? 4
How many legs in all? 12

How many birds? 5
How many legs on each bird? 2
How many legs in all? 10

Page 91

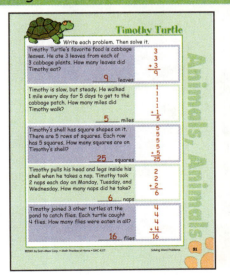

Timothy Turtle

Write each problem. Then solve it.

Timothy Turtle's favorite food is cabbage leaves. He ate 3 leaves from each of 3 cabbage plants. How many leaves did Timothy eat?
3 + 3 + 3 = **9** leaves

Timothy is slow, but steady. He walked 1 mile every day for 5 days to get to the cabbage patch. How many miles did Timothy walk?
1 + 1 + 1 + 1 + 1 = **5** miles

Timothy's shell has square shapes on it. There are 5 rows of squares. Each row has 5 squares. How many squares are on Timothy's shell?
5 + 5 + 5 + 5 + 5 = **25** squares

Timothy pulls his head and legs inside his shell when he takes a nap. Timothy took 2 naps each day on Monday, Tuesday, and Wednesday. How many naps did he take?
2 + 2 + 2 = **6** naps

Timothy joined 3 other turtles at the pond to catch flies. Each turtle caught 4 flies. How many flies were eaten in all?
4 + 4 + 4 + 4 = **16** flies

Page 92

Home to the Hive

Connect the flowers to help Buzz Bee find his way back to the hive. You must always move to a larger number and in order.

96 — 103 — 139   135
82   186
258   212   449
259   185
316   190
370   438   450
381   460
405

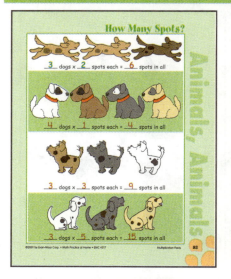

How Many Spots?

<u>3</u> dogs x <u>2</u> spots each = <u>6</u> spots in all

<u>4</u> dogs x <u>1</u> spots each = <u>4</u> spots in all

<u>3</u> dogs x <u>3</u> spots each = <u>9</u> spots in all

<u>3</u> dogs x <u>5</u> spots each = <u>15</u> spots in all

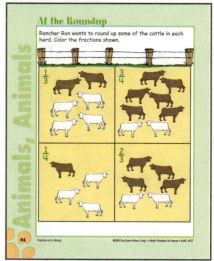

At the Roundup

Rancher Ron wants to round up some of the cattle in each herd. Color the fractions shown.

1/3   3/4

1/4   2/3

Counting Elephants

How many tails?
4 elephants, 1 tail each
<u>4</u> x <u>1</u> = <u>4</u> tails

How many ears?
<u>4</u> elephants, <u>2</u> ears each
<u>4</u> x <u>2</u> = <u>8</u> ears

How many legs?
<u>4</u> elephants, <u>4</u> legs each
<u>4</u> x <u>4</u> = <u>16</u> legs

How many tusks?
<u>4</u> elephants, <u>0</u> tusks each
<u>4</u> x <u>0</u> = <u>0</u> tusks

How many trunks?
<u>4</u> elephants, <u>1</u> trunks each
<u>4</u> x <u>1</u> = <u>4</u> trunks

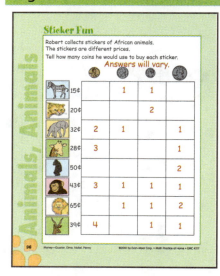

Sticker Fun

Robert collects stickers of African animals. The stickers are different prices. Tell how many coins he would use to buy each sticker.

Answers will vary.

15¢		1	1	
20¢			2	
32¢	2	1		1
28¢	3			1
50¢			2	
43¢	3			1
65¢		1	1	2
39¢	4		1	1

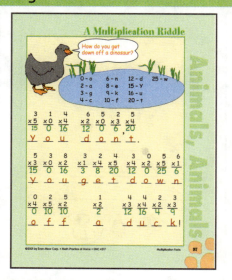

A Multiplication Riddle

How do you get down off a dinosaur?

0 - o	6 - n	12 - d	25 - w
2 - a	8 - e	15 - Y	
3 - g	9 - k	16 - u	
4 - c	10 - f	20 - t	

3	1	0	4	6	5	2	5
x5	x0	x4		x2	x0	x3	x4
15	0	0	16	12	0	6	20
Y	o	u		d	o	n	t.

5	3	8	3	2	4	3	0	5	6
x3	x0	x2	x1	x4	x5	x4	x2	x5	x1
15	0	16	3	8	20	12	0	25	6
Y	o	u		g	e	t		d	o	w	n

0	2	5		1		4	4	2	3
x4	x5	x2		x2		x3	x4	x2	x3
0	10	10		2		12	16	4	9
o	f	f		a		d	u	c	k!

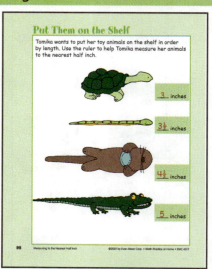

Put Them on the Shelf

Tomika wants to put her toy animals on the shelf in order by length. Use the ruler to help Tomika measure her animals to the nearest half inch.

<u>3</u> inches

<u>3 1/2</u> inches

<u>4 1/2</u> inches

<u>5</u> inches

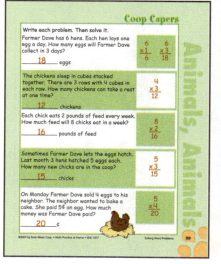

Coop Capers

Write each problem. Then solve it.

Farmer Dave has 6 hens. Each hen lays one egg a day. How many eggs will Farmer Dave collect in 3 days?

6 x1 / 6   6 x3 / 18

<u>18</u> eggs

The chickens sleep in cubes stacked together. There are 3 rows with 4 cubes in each row. How many chickens can take a rest at one time?

4 x3 / 12

<u>12</u> chickens

Each chick eats 2 pounds of feed every week. How much feed will 8 chicks eat in a week?

8 x2 / 16

<u>16</u> pounds of feed

Sometimes Farmer Dave lets the eggs hatch. Last month 3 hens hatched 5 eggs each. How many new chicks are in the coop?

5 x3 / 15

<u>15</u> chicks

On Monday Farmer Dave sold 4 eggs to his neighbor. The neighbor wanted to bake a cake. She paid 5¢ an egg. How much money was Farmer Dave paid?

5 x4 / 20

<u>20</u> ¢

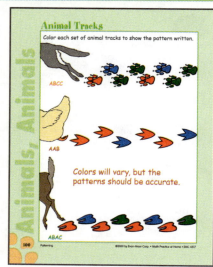

Animal Tracks

Color each set of animal tracks to show the pattern written.

ABCC

AAB

Colors will vary, but the patterns should be accurate.

ABAC

Help the Cows Get Home

Solve the problems. Color the answers in order to show the cows how to get home.

2	4	3	5	6	4	5	2
x3	x2	x3	x1	x0	x3	x5	x2
6	8	9	5	0	12	25	4

2	5	5	6	8	4	9	0
x1	x2	x3	x3	x2	x5	x2	x4
2	10	15	18	16	20	18	0

6	2	6	20	25	16
8	5	12	4	0	9
9	5	0	12	25	6
8	4	15	9	4	3
6	12	15	10	2	8
9	16	18	12	4	10
0	2	16	20	18	0

Page 102

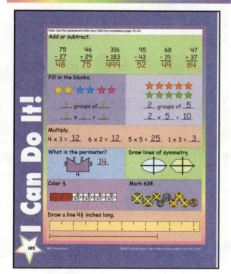

Page 103

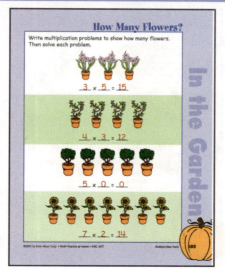

Page 104

Page 105

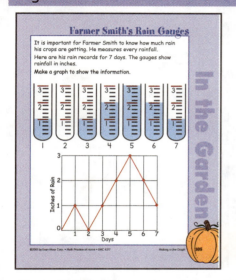

Page 106

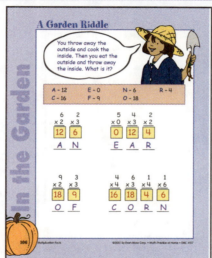

Page 107

Page 108

Page 109

Page 110

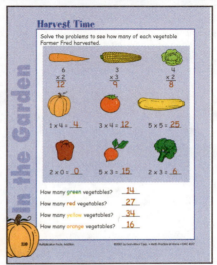

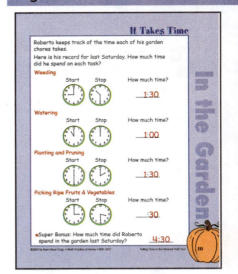

It Takes Time

Roberto keeps track of the time each of his garden chores takes.

Here is his record for last Saturday. How much time did he spend on each task?

Weeding — Start, Stop, How much time? 1:30

Watering — Start, Stop, How much time? 1:00

Planting and Pruning — Start, Stop, How much time? 1:30

Picking Ripe Fruits & Vegetables — Start, Stop, How much time? :30

★Super Bonus: How much time did Roberto spend in the garden last Saturday? 4:30

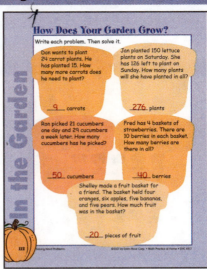

How Does Your Garden Grow?

Write each problem. Then solve it.

Don wants to plant 24 carrot plants. He has planted 15. How many more carrots does he need to plant? — 9 carrots

Jan planted 150 lettuce plants on Saturday. She has 126 left to plant on Sunday. How many plants will she have planted in all? — 276 plants

Ron picked 21 cucumbers one day and 29 cucumbers a week later. How many cucumbers has he picked? — 50 cucumbers

Fred has 4 baskets of strawberries. There are 10 berries in each basket. How many berries are there in all? — 40 berries

Shelley made a fruit basket for a friend. The basket held four oranges, six apples, five bananas, and five pears. How much fruit was in the basket? — 20 pieces of fruit

Gardening Patterns

Every gardener has a way they like to plant the rows in their gardens. Look at each gardener's pattern and label it.

A B C A B C

A A A B B A A A B B

A B B C A B B C

How would you plant your garden? Draw and label your pattern.

Answers will vary.

Apples to Apples

2 sets of 4 apples
2 × 4 = 8

4 sets of 2 apples
4 × 2 = 8

1 set of 6 apples
1 × 6 = 6

6 sets of 1 apple
6 × 1 = 6

3 sets of 4 apples
3 × 4 = 12

4 sets of 3 apples
4 × 3 = 12

Does the number order in multiplication change the answer? — No

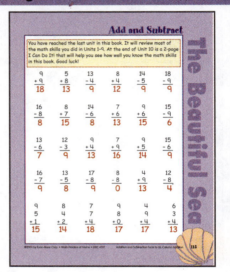

Add and Subtract

You have reached the last unit in this book. It will review most of the math skills you did in Units 1–9. At the end of Unit 10 is a 2-page I Can Do It! that will help you see how well you know the math skills in this book. Good luck!

5	5	13	8	14	18
+9	+8	-4	+4	-5	-9
18	13	9	12	9	9

16	8	14	7	9	15
-8	+7	-6	+6	+6	-9
8	15	8	13	15	6

13	12	9	7	9	11
-6	-3	+4	+9	+5	-6
7	9	13	16	14	9

16	13	17	8	4	12
-7	-5	-8	-8	+9	-8
9	8	9	0	13	4

9	8	7	9	4	6
+1	+2	+4	+8	+4	+4
15	14	17	17	17	13

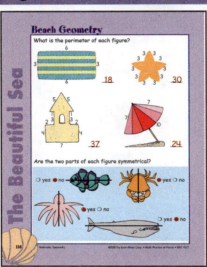

Beach Geometry

What is the perimeter of each figure?

18   30   37   24

Are the two parts of each figure symmetrical?

○ yes ● no   ● yes ○ no   ○ yes ● no (crab / starfish answers)

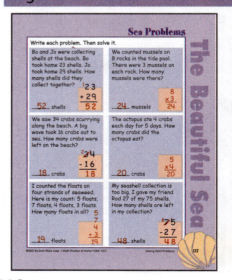

Sea Problems

Write each problem. Then solve it.

Bo and Jo were collecting shells at the beach. Bo took home 23 shells. Jo took home 29 shells. How many shells did they collect together?
23 + 29 = 52 shells

We counted mussels on 8 rocks in the tide pool. There were 3 mussels on each rock. How many mussels were there?
8 × 3 = 24 mussels

We saw 34 crabs scurrying along the beach. A big wave took 16 crabs out to sea. How many crabs were left on the beach?
34 − 16 = 18 crabs

The octopus ate 4 crabs each day for 5 days. How many crabs did the octopus eat?
5 × 4 = 20 crabs

I counted the floats on four strands of seaweed. Here is my count: 5 floats, 7 floats, 4 floats, 3 floats. How many floats in all?
5 + 7 + 4 + 3 = 19 floats

My seashell collection is too big. I gave my friend Rod 27 of my 75 shells. How many shells are left in my collection?
75 − 27 = 48 shells

Measurement Review

A bat ray measures 30 inches across. About how many centimeters would it measure?
○ 30 ○ 25 ○ 15 ● 75

I measured the height of my sandcastle in both inches and centimeters. Which measurement would show the larger number of units?
○ inches ● centimeters

A sea snail crawled 24 inches in 15 minutes. About how far would that be in centimeters?
○ 30 ● 60 ○ 25 ○ 40

A shell is 5 centimeters long. About how many inches is that? (Look at the rulers below.) About 2 inches.

Inches

Centimeters

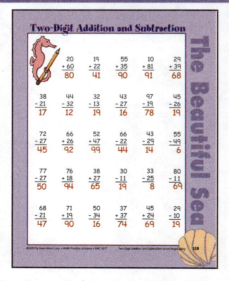

Two-Digit Addition and Subtraction

20	19	55	10	29
+60	+22	+35	+81	+39
80	41	90	91	68

38	44	32	43	97	45
-21	-32	-13	-27	-19	-26
17	12	19	16	78	19

72	66	52	66	43	55
-27	+26	+47	-22	-29	-49
45	92	99	44	14	6

77	76	38	30	33	80
-27	+18	+27	-11	-25	-11
50	94	65	19	8	69

68	71	50	37	45	29
-21	+19	-34	+37	+24	-10
47	90	16	74	69	19

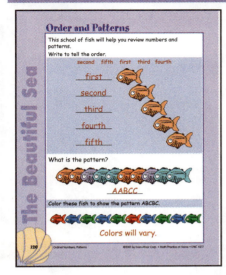

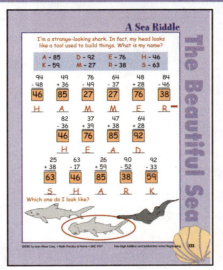

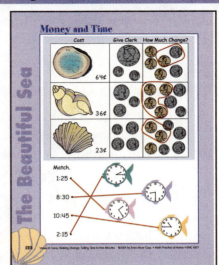

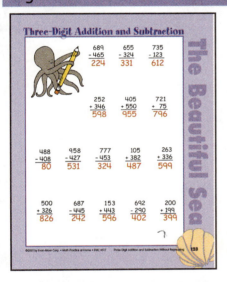

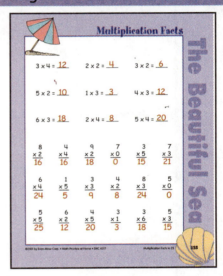

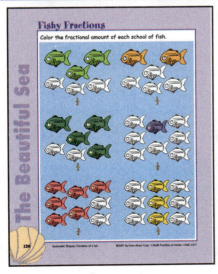

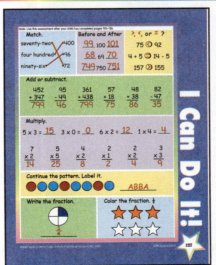

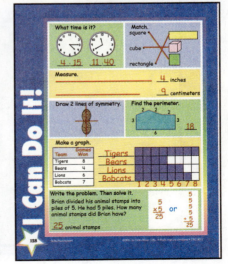

Flash Cards

How to Use the Cards

• Show your child a card. If the answer comes quickly, your child has memorized the combination. Keep the cards your child knows in a separate envelope for periodic review.

• If the answer is slow in coming, allow your child to use counters to figure out the answer. Practice these combinations until they have been memorized.

• Use your creativity to invent games that make flash card study more fun—for example, matching cards with the same answer, laying out a line of cards with answers of 1 through 10 in order, or finding cards in the same number family (e.g., 8 + 7, 7 + 8, 15 − 7, 15 − 8).

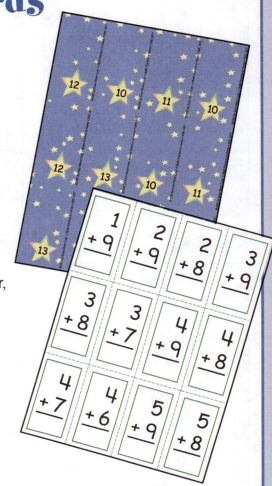

1 + 9 ___	2 + 9 ___	2 + 8 ___	3 + 9 ___
3 + 8 ___	3 + 7 ___	4 + 9 ___	4 + 8 ___
4 + 7 ___	4 + 6 ___	5 + 9 ___	5 + 8 ___

5 + 7 ___	5 + 6 ___	5 + 5 ___	6 + 9 ___
6 + 8 ___	6 + 7 ___	6 + 6 ___	6 + 5 ___
6 + 4 ___	7 + 9 ___	7 + 8 ___	7 + 7 ___

7 + 6 ——	7 + 5 ——	7 + 4 ——	7 + 3 ——
8 + 9 ——	8 + 8 ——	8 + 7 ——	8 + 6 ——
8 + 5 ——	8 + 4 ——	8 + 3 ——	8 + 2 ——

9 + 9 ___	9 + 8 ___	9 + 7 ___	9 + 6 ___
9 + 5 ___	9 + 4 ___	9 + 3 ___	9 + 2 ___
9 + 1 ___	10 + 5 ___	10 + 9 ___	10 + 0 ___

14	13	12	11
− 8	− 8	− 8	− 8

10	16	15	14
− 8	− 7	− 7	− 7

13	12	11	10
− 7	− 7	− 7	− 7

18 - 9 ___	17 - 9 ___	16 - 9 ___	15 - 9 ___
14 - 9 ___	13 - 9 ___	12 - 9 ___	11 - 9 ___
10 - 9 ___	17 - 8 ___	16 - 8 ___	15 - 8 ___

15	14	13	12
− 6	− 6	− 6	− 6

11	10	14	13
− 6	− 6	− 5	− 5

12	11	10	13
− 5	− 5	− 5	− 4

12 − 4	11 − 4	10 − 4	12 − 3
11 − 3	10 − 3	11 − 2	10 − 2
10 − 1	10 −10	10 − 0	18 −18